FROM Microsoft® FrontPage® TO Macromedia® Dreamweaver®

FROM Microsoft® FrontPage® TO Macromedia® Dreamweaver®

JOSEPH LOWERY

201 West 103rd Street, Indianapolis, Indiana 46290

From FrontPage® to Dreamweaver®

Copyright © 2002 by Que Corporation

All rights reserved. No part of this book shall be reproduced, stored in a retrieval system, or transmitted by any means, electronic, mechanical, photocopying, recording, or otherwise, without written permission from the publisher. No patent liability is assumed with respect to the use of the information contained herein. Although every precaution has been taken in the preparation of this book, the publisher and author assume no responsibility for errors or omissions. Nor is any liability assumed for damages resulting from the use of the information contained herein.

International Standard Book Number: 0-7897-2688-2

Library of Congress Catalog Card Number: 20012096311

Printed in the United States of America

First Printing: December, 2001

04 03 02 01   4 3 2 1

Trademarks

All terms mentioned in this book that are known to be trademarks or service marks have been appropriately capitalized. Que Corporation cannot attest to the accuracy of this information. Use of a term in this book should not be regarded as affecting the validity of any trademark or service mark.

FrontPage is a registered trademark of Microsoft Corporation.

Dreamweaver is a registered trademark of Macromedia, Inc.

Warning and Disclaimer

Every effort has been made to make this book as complete and as accurate as possible, but no warranty or fitness is implied. The information provided is on an "as is" basis. The author and the publisher shall have neither liability nor responsibility to any person or entity with respect to any loss or damages arising from the information contained in this book or from the use of the CD or programs accompanying it.

Executive Editor
Jeff Schultz

Development Editor
Laura Norman

Managing Editor
Thomas F. Hayes

Project Editor
Tonya Simpson

Copy Editor
Laura Bulcher

Indexer
Kelly Castell

Proofreaders
Maribeth Echard
Plan-It Publishing

Technical Editor
Derren Whiteman

Team Coordinator
Sharry Lee Gregory

Media Developer
Magnet Media Films

Interior Designer
Gary Adair

Cover Designer
Alan Clements

Page Layout
Stacey Richwine-DeRome
Gloria Schurick

Dedication

*For everyone who ever thought, "There's got to be
a better way"—and then went out and found it.*

Table of Contents

	Introduction	1
1	Introduction to the Interface	3
2	Defining a Site	19
3	Working with Text	31
4	Adding Images	53
5	Creating Links	73
6	Using Layout View	79
7	Previewing Your Page	87
8	Adding Interactivity	93
9	Including Library Items	99
10	Using Templates and Reports	105
11	Publishing Web Pages with Dreamweaver	115
12	Extending Dreamweaver	121
	Glossary	127
A	Keyboard Shortcuts	141
B	What's on the CD	145
	Index	147

About the Author

Joseph Lowery is the author of the *Dreamweaver Bible* and the *Fireworks Bible* series, as well as the *Dreamweaver UltraDev 4 Bible*. His books are international bestsellers, having sold more than 200,000 copies worldwide in nine different languages. Joseph is also a consultant and trainer, and has presented at Seybold in Boston and San Francisco, Macromedia UCON in the United States and Europe, and at ThunderLizard's Web World. As a partner in Deva Associates LLC, Joseph developed for Dreamweaver a set of navigational extensions called the Deva Tools.

Acknowledgments

My heartfelt thanks go out to

- The folks at Magnet Media for getting the ball rolling with the training CD-ROM.
- Eric Ott, former Product Manager for Dreamweaver, for all his feedback and advice.
- Jeff Schultz, for seeing the worth in this book, and Laura Norman, for helping to bring that value to the surface.
- Derren Whiteman, my technical editor, for bringing clarity to both text and image.

FOREWORD

We at Macromedia are pleased you've made the leap from FrontPage to Dreamweaver and we're here to help you make a smooth transition. FrontPage, as a beginning Web page authoring program, definitely serves a purpose. However, many Web developers—perhaps like you—have found that their needs have outgrown what FrontPage can provide and, consequently, have turned to Dreamweaver to be their professional Web design tool.

Dreamweaver was built from the ground up with professional Web production in mind. The expert coders who construct today's leading sites demand a high degree of control over their final product—and they find it in Dreamweaver's Roundtrip HTML ability. With Roundtrip HTML, Dreamweaver honors both the look of a page and its underlying structure, in a restriction-free environment. You're not tied to any one technology in Dreamweaver; moreover, Dreamweaver's extensible architecture ensures that you always have access to the cutting edge.

Dreamweaver's extensibility is one of the most compelling features of the program—in fact, it could more properly be called a feature that builds features. Through its extensibility layer much of Dreamweaver's productivity can be automated and—perhaps more importantly—the basic featureset expanded. It is this capability that allows Macromedia to offer extensions that help Dreamweaver work like FrontPage. With the aid of the FrontPage Migration Kit extensions, you can easily transfer files to and from a FrontPage server, run FrontPage-like reports, and more. As Joe points out in this book, you'll find all of these extensions—and hundreds more—on the Dreamweaver Exchange (*www.macromedia.com/exchange/dreamweaver*).

For all of its raw power, Dreamweaver can't be beat for use of use. The Layout View, new in Dreamweaver 4, greatly simplifies page composition: You can literally draw out a cleanly coded Web page in just minutes. Dreamweaver's integration with other Macromedia products, such as Flash and Fireworks, makes including rich media navigation elements such as

Flash Buttons with animation and sound a drag-and-drop affair. Dreamweaver Behaviors allow you to incorporate elaborate JavaScript interactive effects without knowing a single bit of code.

Dreamweaver is blessed with an extraordinary support system. Not only is there a wealth of information available in the online help systems and tutorials built in to Dreamweaver, you'll also find a wide range of Tech Notes on the Dreamweaver Support Center (*www.macromedia.com/support/dreamweaver*). Tech Notes are extremely helpful when troubleshooting a problem within Dreamweaver or on your Web pages; the Dreamweaver Tech Notes also offer numerous intermediate and advanced Web page production techniques. The Dreamweaver newsgroup (*news://macromedia.dreamweaver*) is another remarkable resource. With a lively roster of leading Dreamweaver designers and Macromedia support personnel fielding an average of 600 posts per day, you'll be sure to find the specific help you need, fast.

I'd like to thank Joe for providing this helpful guide to Dreamweaver for former FrontPage users in both book and CD-ROM training formats. Joe has been chronicling Dreamweaver's path from the beginning; when it comes to Web design and Dreamweaver, Joe Lowery is the expert's expert.

Macromedia is committed to maintaining Dreamweaver's edge as the professional's Web authoring tool of choice. If there is a feature you'd like to see in a future version of Dreamweaver, please let us know by sending an e-mail to *wish-dreamweaver@macromedia.com*. We're looking forward to seeing what dreams you can weave, on the Web.

Diana Smedley

Director of Product Management, Macromedia

Tell Us What You Think!

As the reader of this book, *you* are our most important critic and commentator. We value your opinion and want to know what we're doing right, what we could do better, what areas you'd like to see us publish in, and any other words of wisdom you're willing to pass our way.

As an executive editor for Que, I welcome your comments. You can fax, e-mail, or write me directly to let me know what you did or didn't like about this book—as well as what we can do to make our books stronger.

Please note that I cannot help you with technical problems related to the topic of this book, and that due to the high volume of mail I receive, I might not be able to reply to every message.

When you write, please be sure to include this book's title and author as well as your name and phone or fax number. I will carefully review your comments and share them with the author and editors who worked on the book.

Fax:	317-581-4666
E-Mail:	*ctfeedback@quepublishing.com*
Mail:	Jeff Schultz
	Que Corporation
	201 West 103rd Street
	Indianapolis, IN 46290 USA

INTRODUCTION

Welcome to Dreamweaver

If you've recently made the move from using FrontPage to Dreamweaver—or are planning such a change—this book is for you. Although the two programs share the common goal of creating Web sites, many of the particulars on how that goal is reached are different for Dreamweaver and FrontPage.

This book is designed to ease your transition into Dreamweaver while providing a general introduction to its use. Special focus has been given to the extensions created by Macromedia specifically to help FrontPage users. These extensions are covered in Chapter 2, "Defining a Site," and are available on Macromedia Exchange (*www.macromedia.com/exchange/dreamweaver*); you also can download them by selecting the link from this book's CD-ROM.

All the basics of Web design are covered here: setting up a site, entering text, adding images, establishing links, and more. You'll also find coverage of many of the features that make Dreamweaver the world's leading Web authoring tool, including Cascading Style Sheet support, prewritten JavaScript behaviors, updatable Library items, and templates. You'll even learn how to use some of Dreamweaver's integration capabilities with Flash and Fireworks.

HTML—Dreamweaver's basic language—is used throughout the book rather than FrontPage's proprietary terminology. You'll find a handy FrontPage-to-Dreamweaver jargon guide inside the back cover.

As you work through the exercises in this book, you'll find references to specific documents to use as examples. Each chapter has its own Media folder containing the examples and support files. You can download these examples from my resource site (*www.fp2dw.com*) or by selecting the link found on the CD-ROM that accompanies this book.

You will find helpful tips and notes throughout the book that give you additional insight into the topics being discussed. You'll also find that I provide keyboard shortcuts wherever they apply. The Macintosh shortcut is listed first in parentheses followed by the Windows shortcut in brackets.

The Companion CD-ROM

As an added bonus, this book provides a companion CD-ROM produced by Magnet Media Films and contains a video tutorial where I offer a hands-on approach to moving Web site design projects from FrontPage to Macromedia's Dreamweaver 4. The tutorial will introduce you to the interface and site definitions, show you how to add images, create links, use layout view, add interactivity, use templates and reports, publish your page, and extend Dreamweaver quickly and easily.

You have received the first hyperCD of a two-hyperCD set from Magnet Media, which delivers broadcast quality video along with Internet-based graphics and resources that will be continuously updated so you can keep coming back to learn new features. The training provided on this CD-ROM runs approximately one hour and can be viewed immediately. If you like the training and want to continue with the rest of the material, you can use the CD-ROM link to Magnet Media's site to upgrade online and access additional training. After you upgrade to the additional training, Magnet Media will send you a second hyperCD that contains another hour of training.

CHAPTER 1

Introduction to the Interface

Starting Dreamweaver

Let's dive right into Dreamweaver and take a look around. You'll notice right away that Dreamweaver is pretty sparse to begin with: As shown in Figure 1.1, there's a large open area, called the Document Window, a couple of floating panels, and a Status bar along the bottom. The emphasis here is on your Web page—Dreamweaver keeps all the tools hidden until you need them so that you can focus on your design.

The Document Window has a full menu bar across the top—all program options can be found there, if necessary. I say "if necessary" because Dreamweaver gives you many ways to access program functions: keyboard shortcuts, context-sensitive menus, and a wide range of inspectors and panels. I'll be referring to these alternative methods throughout the book; the more you can incorporate a keyboard or other shortcut, the faster you'll work.

What You'll Learn in This Chapter:
- ▶ All about the Dreamweaver interface and tools
- ▶ How to combine code and design with roundtrip HTML
- ▶ How to customize Dreamweaver and how to get help when you need it

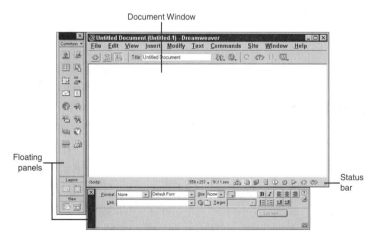

Figure 1.1
Consider Dreamweaver's Document Window your blank Web page canvas.

You'll also notice a feature that is new to Dreamweaver 4's Document Window—the Toolbar. The Dreamweaver toolbar is different from the ones found in FrontPage. You'll find, in comparison, that the Dreamweaver toolbar is much more focused on Web design and production. Not only does the Dreamweaver toolbar allow easy entry of the Web page's title, it also allows you to switch quickly between Design and Code view, or see both at once with Split view.

Combining Code and Design with Roundtrip HTML

A Web page is a blend of artistry and technical expertise; or put another way, a combination of layout and code. Dreamweaver allows you simultaneous and equal access to both sides of the Web page equation through its integrated layout and code editors. This split view brings one notable benefit for novice Web page designers—you can visually place an element, such as an image, and immediately see the HTML tag written for you, thus learning by example. Dreamweaver calls this back-and-forth journey from layout to code *Roundtrip HTML*.

Roundtrip HTML is more than a feature—it's an underlying philosophy of Dreamweaver. With Roundtrip HTML, you don't have to worry about Dreamweaver needlessly modifying your code. Dreamweaver extends this Roundtrip philosophy to server-side code as well, such as that found on ASP, ColdFusion, or PHP pages.

To see the Roundtrip HTML in action, let's go into split-screen mode by choosing the toolbar's second button, Show Code and Design View, shown in Figure 1.2. The code visible in the Code view portion of the screen is always present when Dreamweaver starts. Now, with your cursor at the top of the Document Window, in Design view, type in a line of text, such as *Welcome to Dreamweaver!*. Notice that the code is entered in the Code view simultaneously. If you select any of the text, the code equivalent is also selected.

INTRODUCTION TO THE INTERFACE

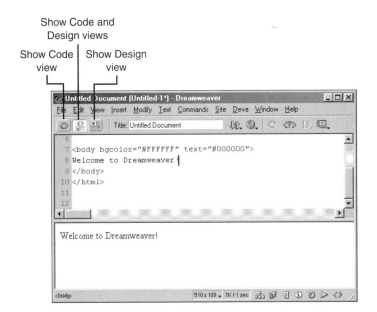

Figure 1.2
Dreamweaver can display both Code and Design views simultaneously.

Keeping Code view open while you work on your Web page is a great way to familiarize yourself with HTML.

Now, try the reverse. Click in the Code view window, immediately following your line of text. Notice how the Code view window is now selected. Next, enter some additional text, such as *Power Web Publishing*. You'll see that the text is not entered at the same time. Click back in the Design view window to see the updated page. Dreamweaver delays the updating of the Design view to allow you to enter complete HTML. You can, however, select text in Code view and see it selected live in Design view.

Using the Status Bar

Located along the bottom of the Document Window, as seen in Figure 1.3, the Status bar has several key functions.

Figure 1.3
Dreamweaver's Status Bar offers rapid selection and access to tools.

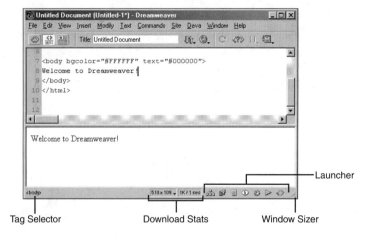

From left to right on the Status bar you'll find

- **Tag Selector**—Displays the current HTML tags, according to the position of the cursor. The Tag Selector is a very useful tool for quickly locating and choosing the right tag.

- **Window Sizer**—Sets and displays the size of the Document Window; excellent when you're designing for a specific page size or checking your design in different sizes of windows.

- **Download Stats**—Shows the current size of the page in kilobytes and approximate download time. Web designers must keep an eye on these figures to make sure the page does not get too heavy in terms of file size and, thus, take too long to download.

- **Launcher**—Opens and closes Dreamweaver's panels. The Launcher is completely user-configurable and you can determine which icons appear in the Status bar or on the larger floating panel.

The Tag Selector

To experience the Status bar in action, open the page *StatusBar.htm* from this chapter folder. In Dreamweaver, choose File→Open and then navigate to the file to select it. When you have it open, follow these steps:

1. Place your cursor anywhere in the first headline and look at the Tag Selector area of the Status bar. You should see two tags, *<body> <h1>*, as shown in Figure 1.4.

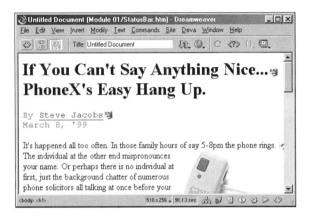

Figure 1.4
HTML tags surrounding the current cursor position are displayed in the Tag Selector area of the Status bar.

2. Select the *<h1>* tag in the Tag Selector and notice how the entire headline is highlighted in the Document Window.

3. Now select the *<body>* tag in the Tag Selector. The entire visible page will be selected; that's because everything in the Document Window is within the HTML *<body>* tag.

Place the cursor in various sections of the page (on the image, for example) to see what tags are displayed in the Tag Selector. Select different tags to see what is highlighted in the Document Window.

The Launcher

Most of Dreamweaver's features are accessible through its floating panels and inspectors. To keep the focus on your Web page, Dreamweaver allows you to open and close these panels with the click of a conveniently located button. The last item on our tour of the Status bar is the control center for Dreamweaver's panels known as the Launcher.

There actually are two Launchers, both of which display identical buttons. The other Launcher is a larger, floating panel invoked by choosing Window→Launcher. Although it's one of the top three choices under the Window menu, I don't favor its use. The Status bar Launcher, seen in Figure 1.5, is much more convenient because it is always available and doesn't get in your way.

Figure 1.5
Open and close your most frequently used tools from the Launcher.

Note
The Launcher panel is totally customizable—you'll see how later in this chapter.

To select any of the panels represented on the Launcher, just click its icon. The panel will appear—or, if already on screen, be brought to the front. Selecting a panel's icon again closes the panel.

Try selecting the panels one at a time, opening and closing them, to familiarize yourself with the interface. The goal is to make choosing the desired panel second nature to you.

The Property Inspector

The Property inspector is Dreamweaver's main method of changing the attributes of a selected element, such as a picture or some text. Many of the features found on FrontPage's Formatting toolbar are duplicated in Dreamweaver's Property inspector. Display the Property inspector by choosing Window→Properties or pressing (Command-F3) [Ctrl+F3]. The Property inspector is context-sensitive and will contain different content depending on what is selected.

The most common attributes for a particular object are found on the upper half of the Property inspector. A small expander arrow opens the Property inspector to full height (see Figure 1.6). Double-clicking in any blank, gray space toggles the Property inspector between half and fully open.

Figure 1.6
Dreamweaver's Property inspector offers easy access to a selected object's attributes.

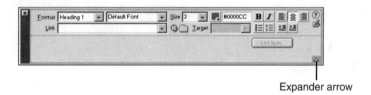

Expander arrow

In addition to text fields, drop-down lists, and on/off buttons, the Property inspector has a couple of unique features:

- **Color Swatch**—Place your cursor so the Text Property inspector is displayed, and click the square (with the down triangle in the corner) to the right of the Size list to open the text color swatch. The 216 colors available are all Web-safe—meaning that both Netscape and Internet Explorer share them. You will notice that your cursor has automatically changed to an eyedropper; click on any color featured in the swatches to select it. You also can move the eyedropper outside the color picker to sample any color on your page. The two buttons on the right side of the color picker are very useful. The first button, a square with a red line through it, is for choosing no color. The second button, a color wheel, opens the operating system's color picker.

- **Folders and Point-to-File Icons**—Next to every text field that requires an external file you'll find a folder and a Point-to-File icon that looks like crosshairs. Click the folder icon to browse to any file available on your system. The Point-to-File icon can be dragged to point to any filename in the Dreamweaver Site window or to any named anchor in the page. (You'll find out about named anchors in the lesson on hyperlinks.)

- **Help**—The encircled question mark actually is a help button that starts your primary browser and opens the Dreamweaver context-sensitive Help Pages.

- **Quick Tag Editor**—Right below the Help button is the new Quick Tag Editor. The Quick Tag Editor allows you to swiftly insert, edit, or wrap HTML around the current selection. It's a great way to tweak your code without having to switch to Code view or open the Code inspector.

To see a few different Property inspectors, open the *StatusBar.htm* file again and click on different objects, such as the text, the image, and the plug-in at the bottom of the page.

The Objects Panel

One of the most often-used of Dreamweaver's floating panels is the Objects panel; choose Window→Objects or press (Command-F2) [Ctrl+F2] to display it. Aside from text, virtually every other element included in an HTML page can be inserted from the Objects panel. This floating panel is slightly different from all others in that it contains several different categories.

To switch from one category to another, select the expander arrow at the top of the Objects panel and choose the desired category from the drop-down list as seen in Figure 1.7.

Figure 1.7
Choose a different object category from the Objects panel list.

The seven standard categories are

- **Common**—The most commonly used objects, including Images, Layers, Tables, Email Link, Tabular Data, Navigation Bar, Date, and several different media types. This panel contains 16 objects in all!

- **Characters**—In HTML, special characters such as ™ and © need to be entered as a unique code. The Characters category offers the Line Break, Non-breaking Space, nine special characters, and an Other Character object for entering any high ASCII entity.

- **Forms**—To gather data from a user, a Web page uses a form and various form elements, all of which can be found in the Forms category.

- **Frames**—A single Web page can be composed of separate HTML documents if frames are used. The Frames category contains an easy way to insert the most commonly used frame layouts (see Figure 1.8).

Figure 1.8
With the Objects panel you can easily include your page in a frameset by applying any of the Frames objects.

- **Head**—An HTML page is made up of two parts: the *<body>*, where all the visible elements of the page are contained, and the *<head>*. The *<head>* section is used for tags relating to the document as a whole, such as *<meta>* tags used to identify the content for search engines. Any object inserted from the Head category is automatically inserted into the *<head>* area, whether it is visible or not.

- **Invisibles**—Three tags, such as the HTML comment tag, are used to lay out or otherwise affect the page, without being visible to the end user. When inserted, these tags are displayed as a symbol that can be selected, moved, or cut and pasted.

- **Special**—The items in this category are separated because they are not actually from the realm of HTML. These objects are used to insert Java applets, ActiveX controls, or items that need plug-ins, such as the QuickTime player.

Let's take a quick look at how the Objects panel is put to use by inserting two different HTML elements—a horizontal line and a special character.

▼ **Try It Yourself**

1. Begin by opening Dreamweaver and choosing Windows→Objects to display the Objects panel if it's not already on-screen.

Note

You also can just click the icon once to insert the object at the current cursor position.

Figure 1.9
Drag Objects panel elements right onto the screen.

2. Be sure you're on the default category of the Object panel, Common.

3. Locate the Insert Horizontal Rule icon and drag it onto the bottom of your page (see Figure 1.9).

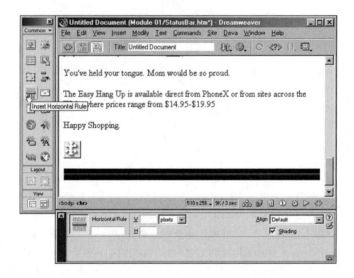

4. If you have the Property inspector open you'll notice that after the horizontal rule is inserted, you can change its properties right away.

5. Click below the rule to deselect it.

6. Enter a copyright line, such as Copyright 2001 BigCo Inc., leaving room for the copyright symbol.

7. Switch to the Characters category of the Objects panel.

8. Drag the Insert Copyright icon into position in the copyright phrase.

9. Use your right-arrow key to move to the object's right and add a space.

INTRODUCTION TO THE INTERFACE

10. Finally, center the line by choosing Align Center from the Property inspector as seen in Figure 1.10.

Figure 1.10
You don't have to select a line to center it in Dreamweaver.

Customizing Dreamweaver

▼ Try It Yourself

One of the true strengths of Dreamweaver is the degree to which it can be customized. You can truly make Dreamweaver work the way you want to work, and that can be a major boost to productivity. Many of the options are found under Dreamweaver's Preferences. You can even personalize the Launcher.

To customize the Launcher, follow these steps:

1. Choose Edit→Preferences and select the Panels category from the list on the left of the Preferences dialog box, shown in Figure 1.11.

Figure 1.11
The list at the bottom of the Panels category of Preferences displays the names of the panels that are currently available through the Launcher.

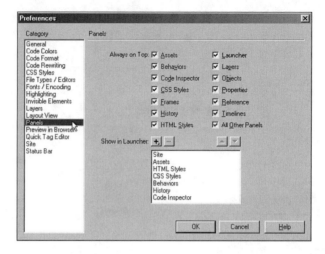

Note

Feel free to explore the other Preferences categories at any time. Most options are placed into effect immediately—there's no need to relaunch Dreamweaver.

2. To add a new panel to the Launcher, select the Add (plus) button and choose any of the available options from the drop-down list.

3. When the panel name is added to the list, you can change its position by selecting it and using the Up and Down arrows. The further up the list, the closer to the left the icons are placed.

4. To remove an icon from the Launcher, select it and click the Delete (minus) button.

Getting Help

Dreamweaver has a lot of depth and, naturally, it takes a while to master all its tools. There is an abundance of help available, however. In addition to a complete online help system, Dreamweaver comes with a series of tutorials, demonstration movies, and a direct connection to Macromedia's support site. Moreover, context-sensitive help is available throughout the program.

It's likely you already have encountered the first bit of Dreamweaver assistance when you started the program. The Welcome panel offers an overview of new features in Dreamweaver 4, guided tours on key steps for using Dreamweaver, as well as links to tutorials and lessons (see Figure 1.12). You can return to the Welcome screen at any time by choosing Welcome from the Help menu.

INTRODUCTION TO THE INTERFACE 15

Figure 1.12
A wealth of tips and tutorials await you in the Welcome panel.

Under the Help menu, you'll also find a link to the Dreamweaver help system, Using Dreamweaver. Using Dreamweaver is a browser-based help system and is accessed by choosing the menu option or the keyboard option (Help) [F1]. Using Dreamweaver opens in your system's default browser, unless you've specified a different one within Dreamweaver.

Once opened, you can click on any one of the topics shown in the Contents pane to reveal the subtopics, as shown in Figure 1.13. Select a subtopic to see the discussion appear in the main frame area. There's also an index as well as a Search feature.

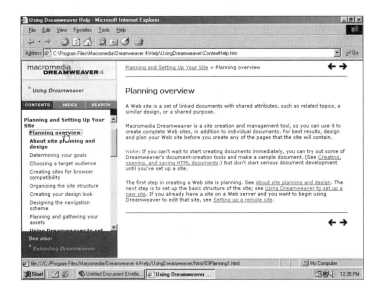

Figure 1.13
The entire Dreamweaver manual is available online through the Dreamweaver Help Pages.

Also under the Help menu are direct links to the Dreamweaver Support Center for up-to-the-moment Technical Notes and to the Dreamweaver Exchange, where additional extensions can be found.

Uncovering Details with the Reference Panel

Although many programs, including FrontPage, have an online help system, few have a built-in reference guide. The world of Web authoring is a detailed and complex one with many different computer languages—including HTML, JavaScript, and others. To help you create properly coded Web pages, Dreamweaver now includes a Reference panel.

For general help, just choose Reference from the Help menu or use the keyboard shortcut, (Command-Shift-F1) [Ctrl+Shift+F1]. This opens the Reference panel seen in Figure 1.14 to one of its three sections: HTML Reference, JavaScript Reference, or CSS Reference. You can switch from one to the other using the Book drop-down menu. Then, you can look up specific tags through the Tag drop-down menu.

Figure 1.14
Get specific code syntax from the Reference panel.

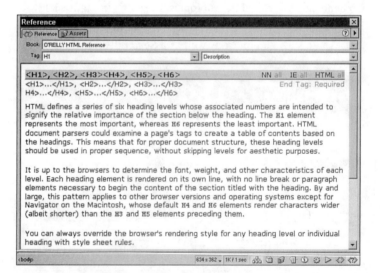

Let's say you want to find out the proper use of the ALT attribute for the *<img>* tag. First, be sure that the Reference panel is set to the HTML Reference. Next, select IMG from the Tag list; finally, choose the ALT attribute.

The Reference panel also can be used contextually. To try this, select the *<hr>* tag from the Tag Selector, and then choose Help→Reference or just press (Command-Shift-F1) [Ctrl+Shift+F1]. The Reference panel opens and displays the entry for the HR tag.

CHAPTER 2

Defining a Site

Installing the Dreamweaver FrontPage Extensions

FrontPage handles site organization—what it calls *Webs*—somewhat differently than the standard implementation of Dreamweaver. Consequently, you'll need to install a few extensions to Dreamweaver, as described in this opening section, before defining a site.

Macromedia includes many useful features in Dreamweaver but, because Dreamweaver is extensible, it's really just the tip of the iceberg as to what's available. If you've ever encountered an out-of-the-ordinary effect on the Web and found yourself thinking, "I wonder how they do that?" there's a good chance a Dreamweaver extension is behind it.

Macromedia has developed a series of extensions designed to help FrontPage users migrate to Dreamweaver. The four extensions are

- **Import FrontPage Site Wizard**—A step-by-step wizard for defining a site in Dreamweaver and importing existing FrontPage Webs.

- **Clean Up FrontPage HTML Sitewide**—Removes unnecessary code added by FrontPage from a single page or an entire site.

- **Site Summary Reports**—Outputs reports familiar to FrontPage users, including reports on File Type, Filter Files by Download Time, Filter by Creation Date, Filter by Modification Date, Hyperlinks, Broken Links, Unlinked Files, and Link Distance.

- **Publish Web Command**—Enables a connection to any FrontPage server from Dreamweaver for publishing a site.

What You'll Learn in This Chapter:
- How to install the FrontPage extensions in Dreamweaver
- How to move your FrontPage Webs to Dreamweaver sites
- All about cleaning up code problems from the converted Webs
- How to create new pages

> **Try It Yourself** ▼

> **Note**
> If you download the extensions from the Dreamweaver Exchange, you'll notice that they have a cataloging prefix starting with the letters MX, combined with the filename. For example, the current version of the FP Site Import extension on the Dreamweaver Exchange is known as *MX254399_FPSiteImport.mxp*. Be aware that the number in the filename changes whenever a new version is released.

> **Figure 2.1**
> The Macromedia Extension Manager is a companion program that can be run from within Dreamweaver or outside of it.

> **Note**
> Remember, you'll have to download this file along with the other extensions from the Web before installing.

All these extensions are available through a link on the CD-ROM. You also can find these—and many more—on the Macromedia Dreamweaver Exchange. The easiest way to connect to this repository is by choosing Help→Dreamweaver Exchange.

Adding extensions to Dreamweaver is fairly straightforward thanks to a helper program, the Extension Manager, that's installed along with Dreamweaver 4. To see how it works, let's install one of the FrontPage extensions:

1. From Dreamweaver, choose Commands→Manage Extensions. This will open up the Macromedia Extension Manager, as shown in Figure 2.1.

   The Extension Manager is divided into two panes: At the top is a listing of all the extensions that have been installed; select one and additional information about that extension is displayed in the lower pane.

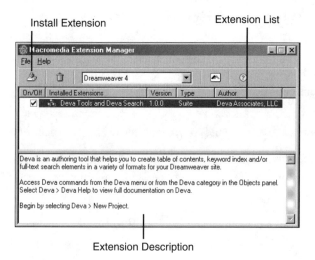

2. Choose the Install Extension button or use the keyboard shortcut, (Command-0) [Ctrl+I]. Whichever method you choose opens up a select file dialog box.

3. Locate the file *FPSiteImport.mxp*, which is the FrontPage Site Wizard. Choose Install when you've found it.

DEFINING A SITE 21

4. The Extensions Disclaimer dialog box opens, allowing you to read through it and then click either Accept or Decline. After you've looked it over, click Accept to install the extension.

5. When the installation is finished, the Extension Manager displays a dialog box to let you know that it's done—and, in this case, that you'll need to restart Dreamweaver. Click OK.

6. Before we relaunch Dreamweaver, locate the newly installed entry, FP Site Import, and select it. In the lower pane, you'll see a brief description and a line indicating how to access the new command.

7. Repeat the procedure to install the three other FrontPage extensions. Their filenames are *CleanUpFPHtml.mxp*, *PublishWebCommand.mxp*, and *SiteSummaryReports.mxp*.

8. Close the Extension Manager, and then quit and restart Dreamweaver.

Setting Up Your FrontPage Web As a Dreamweaver Site

Before we put one of the newly installed extensions to work, let me give you a brief overview of how Dreamweaver handles what FrontPage calls Webs and what, in Dreamweaver, are known as *sites*.

A Dreamweaver site largely is a self-contained entity. All the pages and embedded media usually are kept in one set of folders and subfolders. Dreamweaver manages Web sites by duplicating the structure of the site you created on your local machine to one on a computer set up to serve files over the Internet. For example, if you create a folder called *myWebSite* with two subfolders—one for images and another for scripts—you'll have the same setup on the server: one folder representing *myWebSite* containing two subfolders, *images* and *scripts*. The main folder on your system is called the *local site root folder* and the one on the server is known as the *remote site root folder*.

Note
When installing the additional extensions, the Extension Manager will detect some support files already installed and ask if you want to overwrite them. It's okay to do so.

Try It Yourself ▼

Let's set up a FrontPage Web as a Dreamweaver site, using the FrontPage Site Import extension we previously installed:

1. From Dreamweaver, choose Site→Import FrontPage Site. The FP Site Import Wizard opens, as shown in Figure 2.2.

Figure 2.2
The FP Site Import Wizard steps you through the process of creating the equivalent of a FrontPage Web in Dreamweaver.

2. From the Local Info page of the FP Site Import Wizard, enter whatever you want to call the site within Dreamweaver in the Site Name field. This is the name that appears in Dreamweaver's menus, so pick a name you can easily recognize.

Note

By default, the dialog box looks at the *Inetpub/wwwroot* folder, a common starting point for FrontPage Webs.

3. Click the Browse button to select the folder on your local system that contains the FrontPage Web.

4. Click Select when you've opened the main folder containing the Web.

Caution

It is easy to go one level too deep and open the folder you meant to select. Be sure the folder you want is listed in the Select area in the lower-left portion of the dialog box.

5. Enter the full URL for your site in the HTTP Address text box. The full URL is the address you would enter in a browser to go to your site's home page. Usually it's something like *http://www.bigco.com/*.

6. Click Next when you're ready to move on. The second screen of the wizard, shown in Figure 2.3, is for choosing how you'll connect to your remote Web site.

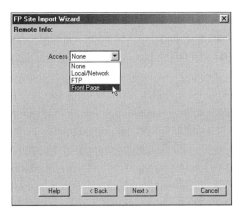

Figure 2.3
Choose FrontPage from the Access drop-down list.

7. From the Access drop-down list on the Remote Info page of the FP Site Import Wizard, choose FrontPage. This is the method you'll use to transfer files to and from your remote site.

Note
There are three standard choices: None, Local/Network, and FTP. If you installed the Publish Web Command, you'll have a fourth option, FrontPage.

8. Click Next to move to the final entry page for the wizard, shown in Figure 2.4.

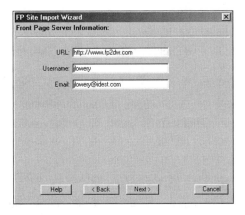

Figure 2.4
You'll enter necessary connection information on the FrontPage Server Information screen.

9. On the FrontPage Server Information page of the wizard, enter the full Internet address for publishing your files in the URL field. This is the same URL you entered in FrontPage when publishing your files.

10. Next, enter your username.

11. Finally, enter your e-mail address. Dreamweaver uses the e-mail address as part of its check-in/check-out system.

12. Click Next to move to the final screen, displayed in Figure 2.5.

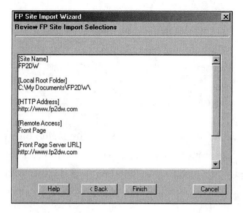

Figure 2.5
After reviewing your choices, make any alterations by selecting Back and navigating to the desired screen.

13. Review your choices made in this wizard. To change anything, press the Back button. If everything looks okay, select Finish. Dreamweaver then tells you the site will be available after a relaunch of the program. Click OK to quit Dreamweaver, or click Cancel to continue using the program.

14. Press OK to close Dreamweaver, and then relaunch it.

15. Upon reopening, you'll get a message indicating that the site has been successfully added. Click OK to continue the startup.

Looking at the Site Window

To see the files in your newly imported site, choose Site→Open Site and then select your site from the list. Dreamweaver's Site window will open, displaying all the files from the FrontPage Web, as shown in Figure 2.6. The Site window is divided into two separate panes. By default, the local file list is on the right and the remote files share the left pane with the Site Map. (I say "by default" because you can switch these views in the Preferences.)

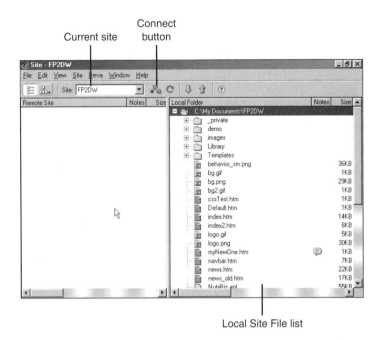

Figure 2.6
After a site is defined, all the available files are listed and ready for use.

Initially, only the local files are listed, including your newly created home page. The remote files will appear after a connection is made to the server. To test that connection, go online, and then select the Connect button in the Site Window. You'll probably need to enter your ISP password at this point. Be sure you select the Save Password option if you want to avoid reentering your password every time you connect to the site.

If the FrontPage information was properly defined, the remote files will appear on the left, as shown in Figure 2.7. If you encounter problems, double-click your site name shown in the Site drop-down list. The Define Sites dialog box will open with all your site information—double-check the values in the Remote Info category before trying the connection again.

Figure 2.7
Click the Connect button to display files on your Remote site.

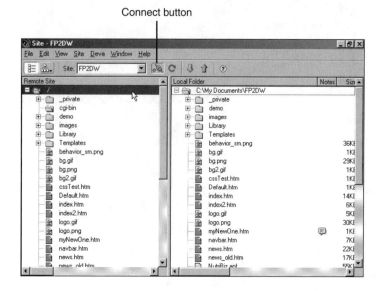

To disconnect from the remote site, click the Connect button again.

You can get a graphic representation of your site by selecting the Site Map button. You can open up any file by double-clicking on its icon in the Site Map or its name in the file list.

Try It Yourself ▼

Cleaning Up FrontPage Code Sitewide

Now that you've set up your site in Dreamweaver with one extension, we'll use another to remove unwanted code from your FrontPage files. The Clean Up FrontPage HTML Sitewide command is capable of eliminating a great deal of FrontPage-specific code that's unnecessary in Dreamweaver and increases file sizes, as well as makes updates more difficult.

If you haven't installed the *CleanupFPHtml.mxp* file yet, go ahead and do that now, following the instructions at the beginning of this chapter.

1. From Dreamweaver, choose Commands→Clean Up FrontPage HTML Sitewide. Dreamweaver's Reports dialog box appears, as displayed in Figure 2.8. You also can access this dialog box by choosing Sites→Reports.

DEFINING A SITE

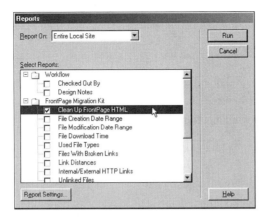

Figure 2.8
The Clean Up FrontPage HTML Sitewide command is actually a Dreamweaver Report.

2. First, select the scope of the cleanup. In this case, I'm going to work on the whole site, so from the Report On list, I'll choose Entire Local Site.

3. Under the FrontPage Migration Kit folder, choose the Clean Up FrontPage HTML option.

4. Click on Report Settings, which has now become available to set the parameters for your cleanup.

5. In the Clean Up FrontPage HTML dialog box (see Figure 2.9), select what you want Dreamweaver to do for each page.

Note
You also have the option to clean up just the current page, any number of files you select in the Site window, or a folder of files.

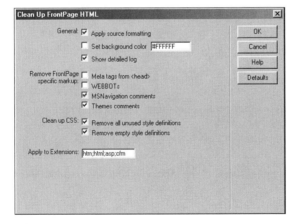

Figure 2.9
To display the Clean Up FrontPage HTML dialog box, select the Report Settings button.

Here are some suggestions:

- I usually select the Apply Source Formatting option because I want to shape the code in the style now set in Dreamweaver. This includes setting the case for tags and their attributes, as well as indenting code for particular tags. The source for any new documents I create in Dreamweaver will have this same formatting, so all my pages will be consistent.

    - In this situation, I know my pages already have a background image, so I'll leave Set Background Color unselected. If needed, I'd enter the desired color in the adjacent field—you can enter a color either in hexadecimal format or using a color name.

    - I like to see what's been done to the various pages, so I almost always select Show Detailed Log.

    - What specific FrontPage markup you opt to remove is entirely up to you and largely depends on where your site is deployed. If you're on a FrontPage server and make use of its various Web bots, I'd leave the boxes for Meta Tags from *<head>* and WEBBOT's unselected. Unless you're planning on reediting the pages in FrontPage, you can safely remove both the MSNavigation and Themes comments.

    - Typically, I'll select both CSS options. CSS is short for Cascading Style Sheets. Although it's a valuable tool in modern Web design, FrontPage often inserts an unnecessary number of CSS definitions and doesn't remove the definitions when the corresponding text is deleted.

    - If you have any file types in addition to HTML, ASP, and ColdFusion that you want to clean up, add their file extensions to the Apply to Extensions field. Be sure to separate each file extension with a semicolon.

6. When you're finished selecting your options, click OK. You won't have to reselect these options again; Dreamweaver will remember your last choices.

7. From the Reports dialog box, select Run to execute the command. You'll get an alert from Dreamweaver letting you know that the command cannot be undone and asking for confirmation to continue. Click OK to proceed.

8. As each page is processed, you'll see an indication of what's happening in the Results dialog box, shown in Figure 2.10. You can open any processed file by double-clicking on its entry or by choosing an entry and selecting Open File.

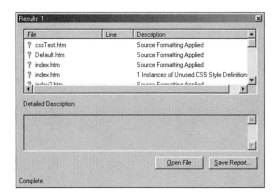

Figure 2.10
The Results dialog box keeps track of all the changes made to your files when you run the Clean Up FrontPage HTML Sitewide command.

9. To keep a report of the Results, choose Save Report. The report is saved in an XML file format that allows it to be presented in any number of ways.

10. Click the Close button to dismiss the Results dialog box when you're finished.

Now that your pages have been cleaned up, you'll find that the code is much easier to follow and, from a professional standpoint, far easier to maintain.

Creating New Pages

Ongoing Web sites are in constant need of maintenance and updates. In addition to modifying existing pages, new pages often will have to be built from scratch. There are several ways to create new pages in Dreamweaver.

From the Document window, choose File→New. This opens a new blank page with the bare bones code necessary for a Web page as shown when looking at the Code view.

You also can create a new page from the Site window in a number of other ways:

- First, you can choose File→New File, which will place an *untitled.htm* file in the file view—ready for you to name.
- You also can use the keyboard shortcut, (Command-Shift-N) [Ctrl+Shift+N], to produce the same effect.
- I like to use the context or shortcut menu whenever possible: (Command) [Right] click in the file view and choose New File from the context menu.

Now that your site is set up and you understand how to create new pages, in the next chapter you'll see how to work with text in Dreamweaver.

CHAPTER 3

Working with Text

Dreamweaver Text Basics

It's no coincidence that text entry is Dreamweaver's default mode. From the minute you boot the program, you're ready to type in new headlines and body text and format them quickly. Although you will find a formatting toolbar like the one used in FrontPage, Dreamweaver's primary method of styling text is through the Property inspector, where you can modify text format, font, size, style, alignment, and more.

By the end of this chapter, you'll even learn about more advanced text techniques, such as Cascading Style Sheets.

Making Headings

As mentioned earlier, the text on HTML pages generally is a combination of headings and regular paragraphs. HTML offers six headings in six relatively different sizes; the key word here is *relative*. The HTML tag for the largest heading size is *<h1>*, followed by *<h2>*, *<h3>*, and so on, to *<h6>*.

It's important to note that, unlike regular page layout programs, HTML headings do not come in specific point sizes. One is relatively larger than the next, but the final on-screen representation is determined by the user's system, particularly their browser. However, in almost all cases, headings appear bold.

To see the different sizes available with basic HTML, follow these steps:

1. Open a new document in Dreamweaver by choosing File→New. Note that the text cursor is already available in the upper-left corner.

What You'll Learn in This Chapter:
- How to work with text in Dreamweaver
- How to format text with the Property Inspector
- How to cut and paste text into Dreamweaver and how to import files from word processors
- All about styling text with HTML styles and CSS

▼ **Try It Yourself**

> **Note**
>
> When you're altering the overall HTML format of a line or paragraph, you don't have to select the text first. This is because the format is applied at the paragraph, not word, level.

Figure 3.1
HTML formats, like Heading 1, affect an entire paragraph.

> **Note**
>
> The text initially will be entered with the same format as the line above it. Format tags are carried over from one line to the next, when you enter a line return.

2. Enter a dummy headline, such as "Heading One." Do not press (Return) [Enter] yet.

3. If it's not already on-screen, open the Property inspector by choosing Windows→Properties.

4. In the Property inspector, choose Heading 1 from the Format drop-down list. Your text should change instantly to a Heading 1, or <h1>, format as seen in Figure 3.1.

5. Press (Return) [Enter] to move to the next line and enter your second heading, such as "Heading Two>."

6. Using the Property inspector, change the Format to Heading 2.

7. Repeat steps 5 and 6, adding new headings and reformatting them, until you have six headings, one for each of the Heading formats. When you're finished, your page should look like Figure 3.2.

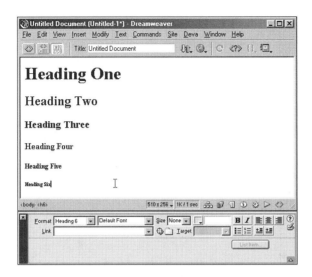

Figure 3.2
Congratulations, you've just created an HTML Headings chart.

8. Save the page by choosing File→Save.

Although Dreamweaver renders Web pages well, it's important to realize that it's not WYSIWYG. Because of all the variables with browsers and systems, it can't be. Preview your page in your primary browser by pressing F12 to see what differences appear between your view in Dreamweaver and the final product viewed in a browser.

Entering Basic Text

Few Web pages can exist on headings alone—it'd be like a newspaper that was all headlines. The main content of a Web page often is found in the regular paragraphs or body copy. In HTML, a paragraph is surrounded by an opening <p> and closing </p> tags, instead of the <h1> through <h6> tags just covered. Browsers automatically word-wrap paragraphs to the size of the browser window; Dreamweaver emulates this wrapping in the Document Window.

To add body text to your Web page, follow these steps:

1. Open the headings page created in the previous exercise by choosing File→Open and locating the document.

2. Place your cursor at the end of the first heading and press (Return) [Enter] to create a new line.

Tip
The keyboard shortcuts for the Heading tags are easy to remember and very useful. Press (Command+1) [Ctrl+1] for <h1>, (Command+2) [Ctrl+2] for <h2>, and so on.

▼ **Try It Yourself**

3. In the Property inspector, change the Format list from Heading 1 to Paragraph.

4. Enter a new paragraph of text.

5. Enter enough text to reach the edge of the Document Window. The text should wrap to the next line, as shown in Figure 3.3.

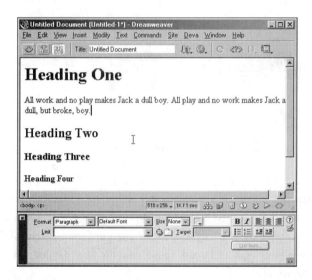

Figure 3.3 Dreamweaver automatically wraps text within the Document Window.

6. When you finish your paragraph, press Enter (Return) again.

7. With your text cursor on the new line, click on the Split code view button on the toolbar. You'll see that the new line looks like this in Code view:

    `<p>  </p>`

The code in between the *<p>* tag pair, * *, is short for nonbreaking space. Dreamweaver automatically inserts a non-breaking space between each new paragraph to keep the line spacing accurate. Without enclosing regular text or a code like * *, browsers would ignore the paragraph tags.

8. Begin to type a new line in the Design view, while keeping an eye on the Code view. At the very first character you type, Dreamweaver erases the no-longer necessary * * code and begins inserting your text.

Note

Note that each paragraph—and heading—is separated by a line of space. This is an HTML convention that adds a blank line between each *block element*. A block element is any paragraph, heading, or other non-inline tag, such as *<blockquote>*. To learn how to place two of the same element types closer together, see the next section on using the line-break tag, *
*.

Browsers compress whitespace to hasten downloads, and only single spaces between sentences and words are preserved. To add additional space, you need to insert a nonbreaking space (like Dreamweaver does initially between the opening and closing paragraph tags). Press (Command+Shift+Space) [Ctrl+Shift+Space] to insert a nonbreaking space.

A blank line normally separates all block elements, such as headings and paragraphs. You can keep lines of the same block element closer together by using a line break tag.

The Line Break Tag:

You've seen how each heading and paragraph is normally given additional space and emphasis by automatically including a blank line on either side of them. But what if you want to have two lines, one right below the other, without the additional space? This effect is achieved with the line break tag, <br>.

To see the effect, place your cursor in the middle of any <h1> line and press (Return) [Enter]. A blank line now divides the two lines. Choose Edit→Undo or use the keyboard shortcut, (Command-Z) [Ctrl+Z], to reverse your last action. Now, press (Shift-Return) [Shift+Enter] instead. One line should be directly beneath the other, as seen in Figure 3.4.

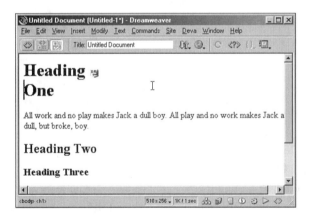

Figure 3.4
The line break tag is very useful for adjusting spacing.

On-Screen Invisible Elements

If you followed the last exercise, you'll notice that Dreamweaver inserts a line break tag at the end of the first line. If you have

Invisible Elements turned on, you can see a small gold shield, representing the *
* tag. If not, choose View→Visual Aids→Invisible Elements to see it.

Now change the format of the current line to any other heading or paragraph. Although the line still breaks at the same point, both the sections before and after the *
* tag are changed. The format affects the whole block element, not just the current line. The *
* symbol in the Document Window doesn't just represent code; you can adjust the placement of the tag by dragging it to a new location or deleting it altogether. All Dreamweaver Invisible Elements work the same way.

You can set which Invisible Elements can be seen in the Document Window by choosing Edit→Preferences and then selecting the Invisible Elements category. Select any or all options available; as shown in Figure 3.5, I prefer to set all of mine on.

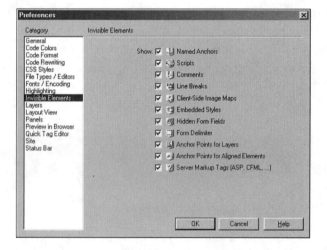

Figure 3.5
Determine which code elements will be represented in the Dreamweaver workspace through the Invisible Elements category of Preferences.

Formatting Text with the Property Inspector

In addition to changing a paragraph's basic format, you also can alter any selected text's font, size, or color. Blocks of text can be aligned left, right, or center, as well as indented on both the left and right margins. In Dreamweaver, all this functionality is found in the Property inspector instead of in a toolbar as in FrontPage.

FrontPage lets you assign any font on your system to any text; unfortunately, the Web doesn't really work that way. In general, Web pages rely on the fonts that are found on the user's own system. To work with different systems, proper HTML—and Dreamweaver—uses *font families* rather than a single font.

To see an example, select any text on your page, either by highlighting it or by selecting a tag from the Tag Selector. Now, in the Property inspector, select the option list where Default Font is currently displayed, as shown in Figure 3.6. Choose the first option: Arial, Helvetica, sans serif. If you are working on a Windows system, the text changes to Arial; on a Macintosh, it becomes Helvetica; and if you have neither of those fonts on your system, a generic sans serif font is used.

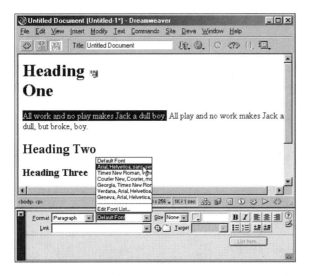

Figure 3.6
Use the Property inspector to quickly change from one font family to another.

Changing Font Size

HTML font sizes are either absolute or relative. Dreamweaver's Property inspector enables you to choose one of seven different explicit sizes that the browser can render (absolute sizing), or you can select one relative to the page's basic font. The *absolute sizes* are numbered 1 through 7, where (unlike the heading sizes) 1 is the smallest and 7 is the largest. *Relative sizes*—not available in FrontPage—have a plus or minus sign in front of them, like +2.

Note

To change the text you just modified to another font, it's best to place your cursor inside the text and select the font tag from the Tag Selector before choosing a new font family. This prevents additional font tags from being added to your code.

Which size type should you use: absolute or relative? Relative sizing gives you additional flexibility because you can resize all the fonts in an entire Web page with one command (changing the *<basefont>* tag) . Absolute sizes, on the other hand, appear more straightforward to use. It's your decision as designer which one to use and when.

Absolute Sizes

Although there's no direct correlation between the print world's point size and the Web world's absolute sizes, they roughly go from 8pt for a size 1 to 36pt for a size 7.

▼ Try It Yourself

To use the Property inspector to pick an absolute font size, follow these steps:

1. Select your text.

2. In the Property inspector, open the Font Size drop-down list of options, as shown in Figure 3.7.

Figure 3.7
You can choose a new size for your selected text from the Font Size list or just type in a value.

3. Choose a value from 1 to 7.

Relative Size

To what, exactly, are relative font sizes relative? The default font size, of course. The advantage of relative font sizes is that you can alter a Web page's default font size with one command, the *<basefont>* tag.

You can distinguish a relative font size from an absolute font size by the plus or minus sign that precedes the value. The relative sizes are plus or minus the current *<basefont>* size. Thus, the tag *<font size=+1>* is normally rendered with a size 4 font, because the default *<basefont>* is 3. If you include in your Web page the following line:

```
<basefont size=5>
```

text marked with *<font size=+1>* is displayed with a size 6 font. Because browsers display only seven different size fonts, with a *<basefont size=5>* setting any relative size over *<font size=+2>* won't display differently when previewed in a browser.

To use the Property inspector to pick a relative font size, follow these steps:

▼ **Try It Yourself**

1. Select your text or position the cursor where you want the new text size to begin.

2. In the Property inspector, open the Font Size drop-down list of options.

3. To increase the size of your text, choose a value from +1 through +7.

4. To decrease the size of your text, choose a value from −1 to −7.

Color

Unless you assign a color to text on your Web page, the browser uses its default, typically black. The overall color for text on the entire page is set by choosing Modify→Page Properties and selecting a new color from the Text Color swatch. Moreover, you also can color any specific headings, characters, words, or paragraphs that you have selected in Dreamweaver. The color swatch control can be found on the Property inspector between the font size list and bold button.

All the color swatch controls in Dreamweaver open the same color picker, shown in Figure 3.8. The color picker includes the 212 colors common to the Macintosh and Windows palettes, know as the browser-safe colors. If you choose a color outside the "safe" range, you have no assurances of how the color is rendered on a viewer's browser. Some systems select the closest color in RGB values; some use dithering (positioning two or more colors next to each other to simulate another color) to try to overcome the limitations of the current screen color depth. So be forewarned: If at all possible, stick with the browser-safe colors, especially when coloring text.

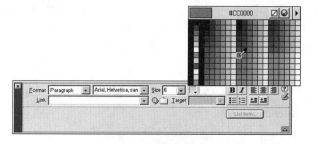

Figure 3.8
You'll find that the same color picker used to choose the Font Color swatch is used throughout Dreamweaver when making color selections.

Try It Yourself

To use the Property inspector to color a range of text in Dreamweaver, follow these steps:

1. Select the text you want to color, or position the cursor where you want the new text color to begin.

2. From the Property inspector, you can

   - Type a hexadecimal color number directly into the Font Color text box.

   - Type a color name directly into the Font Color text box.

   - Select the Font Color swatch to open the browser-safe color picker.

3. If you chose to type a color name or number directly into the Font Color text box, press Tab or click on the Document Window to see the color applied.

4. If you clicked the Font Color swatch, select your color from the browser-safe colors available, as displayed in Figure 3.8.

As you move your pointer over the color swatches, Dreamweaver displays the color in the upper-left corner and the color's hexadecimal value to the right of that.

5. For a wider color selection from the Color dialog box, select the Palette icon in the upper-right corner of the color swatch.

6. If you decide not to apply a different color, click the no color button (the square with the red line through it) to return to using the default color that's assigned in the page properties.

Alignment and Styles

Text alignment in Dreamweaver is almost identical to a traditional word-processing program. Just like a word-processing program, Dreamweaver aligns text one paragraph at a time. You can't left-align one word, center the next, and then right-align the third word in the same paragraph. Moreover, basic HTML only supports the alignment of text to the left or right edge, or in the center of the browser window. You must use Cascading Style Sheets (covered later in this chapter) to justify your text.

To align text, you can use one of three methods: a menu command, the Property inspector, or a keyboard shortcut (see Table 3.1). To use the menus, choose Text→Align and then pick the alignment you prefer (Left, Right, or Center) as shown in Figure 3.9.

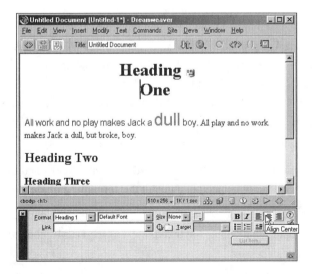

Figure 3.9
In HTML, there are three text alignment choices.

Table 3.1 Keyboard Shortcuts for Aligning Text

Alignment	Window Keyboard Shortcut	Macintosh Keyboard Shortcut
Left	Ctrl+Alt+Shift+L	Command-Option-Shift-L
Center	Ctrl+Alt+Shift+C	Command-Option-Shift-C
Right	Ctrl+Alt+Shift+R	Command-Option-Shift-R

> **Note**
> What, no U for underline? Although you can underline text in HTML, it's not such a great idea. By default, links are underlined, so to avoid confusion, Dreamweaver makes the underline command a little less tempting. But if you really need it, you can find it under the menus, Text→Style→Underline.

Just before the three alignment buttons on the Property inspector, you'll find familiar Bold and Italic buttons. As you might suspect, simply select some text and then click the B, the I, or both.

Cutting and Pasting Text into Dreamweaver

Naturally, you can cut or copy text from any text editor and bring it into Dreamweaver where it's pasted at the current cursor position using (Command-V) [Ctrl+V]. But Dreamweaver—with one exception—only pastes plain, unformatted text.

In order for you to insert HTML code examples in your Web page, Dreamweaver pastes the contents of the clipboard into the document window in whatever format you copied it to the clipboard. That means that if you copy a couple of paragraphs out of a text document, or your word processor, Dreamweaver pastes this as plain text. However, if you copy text with HTML tags, say out of the HTML preview in FrontPage or another text editor, you will see all these tags written out in your document window.

Using Copy As HTML and Paste As HTML

The only problem with this literal pasting of tags is that you might actually have intended for the HTML to become part of your Web page. In this case, you'll need to use Dreamweaver's Paste HTML command instead.

> **Try It Yourself**

To see an example of this, follow these steps:

1. Type a sample heading into the document window and use the Property inspector to give it the formatting of Heading 1.

2. Choose Edit→Copy HTML. As discussed earlier in this chapter, that copies the text as well as the HTML code to your clipboard.

3. Open up an external text editor—Notepad or SimpleText will suffice—and paste the contents of your clipboard there. You'll notice that the HTML tags are written out in the text.

4. Make a small change, and then select that text in your external editor, copy it using (Command-C) [Ctrl+C], and return to Dreamweaver.

5. If you position your cursor in the document window and press (Command-V) [Ctrl+V] to paste the text, you'll notice that you can see the tags again.

6. To paste it as inline code, choose Edit→Paste HTML.

   Now your paragraph is in Dreamweaver and your sample heading has shown up in the Heading 1 format again.

Importing Word Documents

For complex documents that are preformatted, you'll want to preserve as much of the formatting as possible. One route is to use Microsoft Word to convert the file to HTML and then bring the HTML into Dreamweaver. Although this seems like a no-brainer, Microsoft's standard HTML output is very dense—and especially well-formed HTML at that. Redundant tags are the rule rather than the exception and, especially with Word 2000, unnecessary XML tags bloat the document to two or three times its size. Dreamweaver comes to the rescue with its Import Word HTML command.

Not only does Dreamweaver import Word HTML, it cleans it up significantly. HTML files from Microsoft Word 97, Word 98, or Word 2000 are eligible for import. Not only does the cleanup take place automatically upon import, but you can fine-tune the modifications that Dreamweaver makes to the file. When the file is in, you can apply the current Source Format profile so that the HTML is even styled to look like native Dreamweaver code.

Of course, before you can import a Word HTML file, you must have created one. In Word 97/98, to export a document in HTML format you chose File→Save as HTML; in Word 2000, the command has changed to File→Save as Web Page. Although the wording change might seem to be a move toward less jargon, its significance is what Word actually exports. With Word 2000 (and all the Office 2000 products), Microsoft heartily embraces the XML standard and uses a combination of standard HTML and custom XML code throughout their exported Web pages. For example, here's the opening tag from a Word 2000 document, saved as a Web page:

```
<html xmlns:o="urn:schemas-microsoft-com:office:office"
xmlns:w="urn:schemas-microsoft-com:office:word"
xmlns:dt="uuid:C2F41010-65B3-11d1-A29F-00AA00C14882"
xmlns="http://www.w3.org/TR/REC-html40">
```

> **Note**
> There is an upgrade to Office available on the Microsoft Web site called Office HTML Filter 2.0 that allows you to copy any selection as HTML in Word. It's a very useful feature and a highly recommended upgrade.

which Dreamweaver alters to

```
<html>
```

Dreamweaver imports only full documents; in other words, you can't import a Word HTML file in the middle of another Dreamweaver file. You have to import it as its own document and then cut or copy the text in the Document Window and paste it into your page. To get the full page, select the *<body>* tag from the Tag Selector before copying.

Try It Yourself ▼

If you accept the defaults, importing a Word HTML file is very straightforward:

1. Choose File→Import→Import Word HTML. If you don't have a Word HTML document to test, you'll find one included in the Media file for this chapter as *Word Sample.htm*. (For fun, you might want to open the file in Dreamweaver first, and then look at the source code in either Code view or the Code inspector.)

2. The Import Word HTML dialog box opens and Dreamweaver looks to see whether the HTML file was exported from Word 97/98 or 2000 and changes the options accordingly. As can be seen in Figure 3.10, the *Word Sample.htm* file was exported from Word 2000.

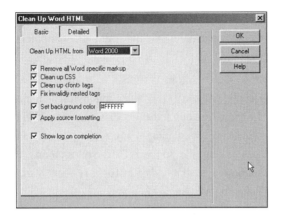

Figure 3.10
Remove unnecessary tags and drastically shorten your download time with the Import Word HTML command.

3. Click OK to confirm the import operation.

   Now, Dreamweaver creates a new HTML document, imports the file, and cleans up the code. If the Show Log on Completion option is selected, Dreamweaver supplies an overview of the modifications made.

For most purposes, accepting the defaults is the best way to quickly bring in your Word HTML files. However, because Web designers have a wide range of code requirements, Dreamweaver provides a full set of options so you can tailor the Word-to-Dreamweaver transformation to your liking. There are actually two different sets of options—one for documents saved from Word 97/98 and one for those saved from Word 2000. The different sets of options can be seen on the Detailed tab of the Import Word HTML dialog box; the Basic tab is the same for both file types. I recommend that you stick with the defaults until you discover a necessary alteration.

Applying HTML Styles

Before we start this part of the lesson, you'll have to include some sample styles to work with. From the Media folder that accompanies this chapter, copy the *styles.xml* file into your site's Library folder. If your site does not have a Library folder yet, you'll need to make one at the site root.

There are two basic types of HTML Styles: paragraph and selection. Paragraph styles are applied to the current paragraph and selection styles to the current selection. Both types of HTML Styles can either replace the existing font tags or supplement them.

The HTML Styles panel lists available styles, as well as provides New Styles and Delete Styles buttons. Paragraph styles appear with a paragraph symbol (¶) and Selection styles with an underlined a, like this: a̲. You can tell the styles that are added to the existing tags instead of replacing them by the plus sign next to the style symbol. For example, in the HTML Styles palette, Red is a standard selection style that adds a `color="#FF0000"` attribute to whatever `<font>` tags exist.

Try It Yourself ▼

To see how you apply an HTML Style, follow these steps:

1. Open the page *HTML_sample.htm* from this chapter's Media folder.

2. Display the HTML Styles panel by selecting its button in the Launcher (a paragraph symbol) or choosing Window→HTML Styles.

3. Be sure the Auto apply option is selected on the HTML Styles panel, as shown in Figure 3.11.

Figure 3.11
Select the Auto apply option to allow quick formatting through the HTML Styles panel.

4. Place your cursor in the first headline on the page that starts "The Online Pharmacy…."

5. From the HTML Styles panel, choose the Headline style. The paragraph is instantly made larger, bold, and in a particular font family. To see exactly what attributes are applied, check the Property inspector.

Try It Yourself ▼

Now, let's try a selection style:

1. Select the first price for a report, $995.

2. From the HTML Styles panel, choose the selection style Emphasis, Sans Serif. Again, the font is changed and bold is added, but this time only to the selection, not to the entire line, as seen in Figure 3.12.

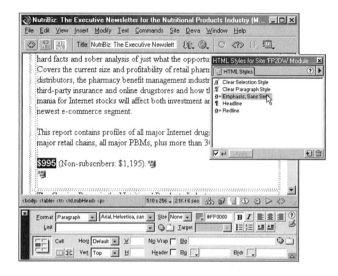

Figure 3.12
You can apply HTML styles to either a full paragraph or some selected text.

Try out the various paragraph and selection styles on different parts of the page. To remove a paragraph style, place your cursor in the formatted line and select Clear Paragraph Style from the HTML Styles panel. To remove a selection style, select the formatted text and choose Clear Selection Style.

It's best to use the Tag Selector to select the formatted text rather than dragging across the text. With the Tag Selector you can be sure to get exactly the format you want to remove.

Styling Text with Cascading Style Sheets

As designed by the W3C (World Wide Web Consortium—the keepers of Web standards) the *Cascading Style Sheets (CSS)* specification is enormously far-reaching. In addition to text formatting, CSS can also precisely position content through layers, highlight text with background colors, and even provide new symbols for bullet lists. Unfortunately, the CSS dream is only on the verge of catching up with the reality of browsers and, currently, I recommend using CSS primarily for manipulating text.

However, even with that limitation, CSS is very powerful—and we're going to start with one of its most powerful forms: the external style sheet. With an *internal style sheet*, you can define CSS styles for any given Web page, and when you change those styles the look is instantly updated—on that page. An *external style sheet*, however, can be linked to any number of pages, even an entire Web site; make one change in an external style sheet and that change is instantly applied to all the linked pages.

Try It Yourself ▼

Let's make an external Cascading Style Sheet:

1. Open the file *css_sample.htm* from this chapter's Media folder.

   Yes, it's almost the same basic file as seen in the HTML Style portion of the lesson. Aside from my unrepentant laziness, I wanted to show you how the two systems work on basically the same file.

2. Open the CSS Styles panel by clicking its button on the Launcher or choosing Window→CSS Styles.

   The CSS Styles panel is used to create, edit, apply, and remove styles (see Figure 3.13).

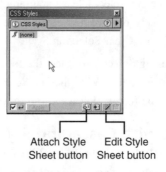

Attach Style　Edit Style
Sheet button　Sheet button

Figure 3.13
The CSS Styles panel lists custom styles you've created.

3. Select the Attach Style Sheet button from the bottom of the CSS Styles panel. The Attach Style Sheet button is on the left of the four-button group.

   The Select Style Sheet File dialog box opens. If a style sheet already existed, we could browse for it. However, we also can create a new one on the spot.

4. In the File name/URL field, enter a name for a new style sheet, like *myStyle.css*, and click select.

   Be sure to add the .css extension to quickly identify your CSS documents.

5. At this point you'll be returned to the document window, where it might seem like nothing has happened. If you look at your page in the Code inspector or in Code view, you'll see that Dreamweaver has indeed inserted a link to the new style sheet. Now it's time to actually define a style for our new sheet. Click the Edit Style Sheet button, on the CSS Styles panel, to open the Edit Style Sheet dialog box.

6. On the Edit Style Sheet dialog box, as shown in Figure 3.14, you'll see a list of styles that you've defined. The new external sheet that we created in step 5 is now in the list window, identified as a (link). Select the *myStyle.css* (link) entry, and then choose the Edit button.

   This opens another, similar Style Sheet dialog box, except this one specifies our file.

Figure 3.14
The Edit Style Sheet dialog box shows defined styles and/or linked style sheets.

7. Select the New button. As noted earlier, you can define a custom style (or class) or redefine an existing HTML tag with CSS; you also can define link attributes, through the CSS Selector. The New Style dialog box allows you to choose what you're going to do. For instant gratification, we're going to redefine an HTML tag.

8. Select the Redefine HTML Tag option, and then find h2 in the drop-down Tag list. Click OK when you're ready. The Style Definition for h2 dialog box that opens is where the real work gets done (see Figure 3.15). We'll just change a few attributes so you see what's possible.

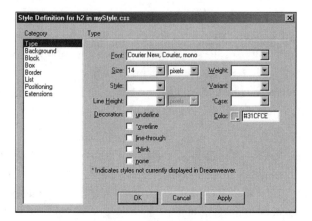

Figure 3.15
Specific style options are selected in the Style Definition dialog box.

9. Make these changes in the Type category:

    - Change the font to Courier New, Courier, mono.

    - Make the size 14 point.

    - Select the Color swatch and sample the dark blue-green color from the document or pick another color.

10. Click OK to close the style definition, click Save to close the Edit *myStyle.css* dialog box, and then click Done to close the Edit Style Sheet dialog box.

You'll notice that both of the <h2> headings are changed to this new format, as shown in Figure 3.16. If the page had had 100 <h2> headings, they too would have been altered. That's the beauty of CSS that you're just starting to explore.

WORKING WITH TEXT

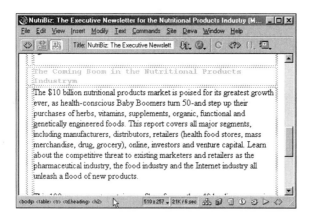

Figure 3.16
When you define an HTML tag through CSS, your changes instantly appear in Dreamweaver.

CHAPTER 4

Adding Images

Images and Dreamweaver

Graphics support is very robust in Dreamweaver. Not only are all three Web format types (GIF, JPEG, and PNG) available for preview and display, but the tight integration with Fireworks makes short work of modifying or optimizing graphics. Dreamweaver also gives you the power to easily create rollover images and manipulate background images. You can even use a tracing image to facilitate laying out your pages.

Formatting images is much simpler in Dreamweaver than in FrontPage. Rather than having to go through a somewhat hidden Properties dialog box, most of a graphic's attributes can be found—and altered—right on the Dreamweaver Property inspector.

Inserting Foreground Images

Graphics on the Web can be divided broadly into two uses: foreground and background. In this section we'll be looking at foreground images.

Because any foreground image can be placed next to another image or in the same line as text, HTML graphics are also called *inline graphics*. In Dreamweaver, a graphic typically is placed on a page by using the Insert Image object, located on the Common category of the Objects panel.

To get the feel of working with Web graphics in Dreamweaver, let's try inserting a couple of images:

1. Start a new page by choosing File→New.

What You'll Learn in This Chapter:
- ▶ How to work with images
- ▶ What the Asset panel and Property Inspector have to do with images
- ▶ How to build a rollover and how to optimize images using Fireworks
- ▶ How to use an image as a background and how to create an image map
- ▶ How to add Flash buttons and Flash text

▼ **Try It Yourself**

2. Select the Insert Image object from the Common category on the Objects panel.

   The Select File dialog box is displayed, as shown in Figure 4.1.

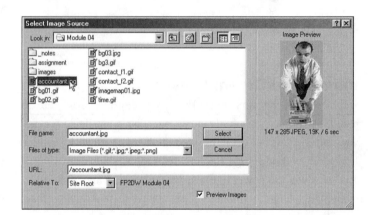

Figure 4.1
The preview option makes picking your graphic file from the Select File dialog box very straightforward.

3. Navigate to the Media folder for this chapter and select the file *accountant.jpg*.

   The Dreamweaver Select File dialog box displays previews for JPEG, GIF, and PNG files as well as important information such as dimensions and file size.

4. Click OK to insert the graphic.

5. If you haven't saved your document (and I purposefully did not tell you to), you'll get a dialog box that tells you a "file://" path will be appended. I recommend—and will remind you—that you always save new files in their intended site first, to avoid issues like these.

   Another dialog box appears if you are not in the currently opened site. This dialog box gives you the opportunity to copy the selected image to your current site. If you agree to, a Copy File As dialog box appears—looking exactly like the Select File dialog box. Navigate to your current site and save the file wherever you'd like.

When the file is first inserted in Dreamweaver, it's still selected and you can see its attributes, if you have the Property inspector open.

6. Press the Right Arrow key to deselect the image and move the cursor next to it.

7. Insert another image by using the keyboard shortcut, (Command-Option-I) [Ctrl+Alt+I].

8. Select the *time.gif* image for your second image. Notice how the second image comes in right next to the first, aligned at the bottom as shown in Figure 4.2. This is the browser default alignment and can be altered, as you'll see later on.

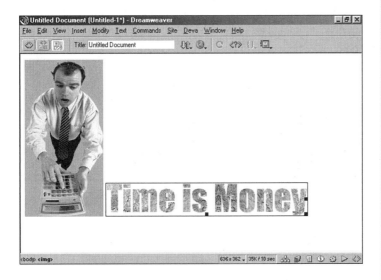

Figure 4.2
In HTML, you can control the vertical alignment between side-by-side images.

9. To separate the two images, select *time.gif*, and then press the left arrow key to move between them.

10. Press (Return) [Enter] to move the second graphic to the next line.

11. To create a smaller vertical gap between the two images, press (Command-Z) [Ctrl+Z] to undo the last action, and then press (Shift-Return) [Shift+Enter] to insert a line break.

Using the Assets Panel

With Dreamweaver 4's Assets panel, inserting graphics, and many other types of objects, just got a whole lot easier. The Assets panel breaks down your Web site components into nine different categories: Images, Colors, URLs, Flash, Shockwave, Movies, Scripts, Templates, and Library. As your site is built, the Assets panel categorizes all of these items and keeps them sorted and ready for you to reuse at any point.

To see your site's assets, and to add something to your document, open the Assets panel by pressing F11 or by choosing Window→Assets. Choose the category for the item you want to insert. Let's choose Images.

Select an item, and then click the Insert button at the bottom of the Assets panel. The graphic is placed on the page at the cursor position, as shown in Figure 4.3.

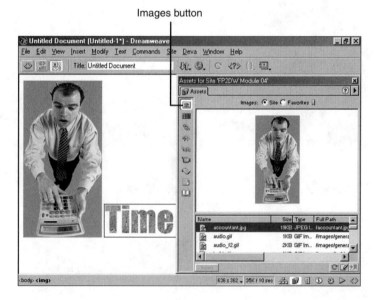

Figure 4.3
The Assets panel is a great way to speed your production.

Another method is to drag an item from the Assets panel into the document window. It will be placed wherever you release your mouse button.

If you have a lot of images, you can sort them in a variety of ways in the Assets panel by selecting a column heading at the top of the list of images.

Modifying Image Attributes in the Property Inspector

When an image is selected in Dreamweaver, the Property inspector displays a host of possible attributes for the image. You can change the image's dimensions, add space around it, give it a border—and, perhaps most importantly, you can assign a link to it.

As can be seen in Figure 4.4, Dreamweaver fills in some of the attributes for you when a graphic is inserted: the source (or src), width (W), and height (H). All of these can, of course, be altered through the Property inspector. You can change an image tag's source (and thus the image) by selecting the folder icon or just double-clicking the image; the Select File dialog box opens in either case.

Figure 4.4
When an image is selected, all its attributes are available through the Property inspector.

Let's take a look at the initial image parameters available on the Property inspector:

- The very first parameter—the image's name—is important for setting up rollovers and other interactive actions. The name box is found just next to the thumbnail on the left side of the Property inspector. Give your image a unique name, if it's going to be used interactively in a rollover or other JavaScript function.

Caution

JavaScript names have particular rules. Use only alphanumeric characters and avoid special characters, including spaces and quotes.

- In addition to altering the Width and Height with the mouse, you can enter new values in the W and H fields, respectively. When you change a value from the original, the W and/or H turn bold; restore the value by selecting the W and/or H or clicking the Refresh button.

To resize an image on-screen, use its sizing handles. After you've selected an image, you'll notice three black boxes, one on the bottom, one on the right, and the third in the bottom-right corner, as shown in Figure 4.5. Drag any of these handles to resize the graphic. If you hold down the Shift key after you've begun dragging the corner handle, the image will resize according to its original height:width aspect ratio.

Figure 4.5
Resize an image in Dreamweaver for layout purposes only; use a graphics editor such as Fireworks or Photoshop to do the actual rescaling.

Note

It's important to note that, when you resize an image in Dreamweaver, you're not changing the file size and you won't get the best results. I use Dreamweaver's resizing capability to find the best size for a graphic and then rescale it in Fireworks. Always use a graphics editor to alter graphic dimensions permanently.

- The Src (source) and Link fields here work the same as the Link field in the Text Property inspector. Enter a new path and filename or use either the Point-to-File or Folder icon to select your src or link.

- Change the alignment of the image by choosing a new option from the Align drop-down list.

- Enter text describing your image in the Alt field.

Whatever you put in the Alt text field is initially shown when a page is loading, and as a pop-up tip when the user's mouse passes over the image. More importantly, the Alt text is what users with text only browsers see and what screen readers read to people with visual disabilities.

The more infrequently used—but also important—attributes are found on the lower half of the Property inspector. Of these attributes, the border and margin controls, vertical space, and horizontal space more typically come into play. Other elements, such as the image map controls and the horizontal alignment, are covered in future chapters. The Edit button is used to send your image to a graphics editor, such as Fireworks.

You can place an outline around any image by entering a pixel size value in the Border field. Open a new page and bring in the *time.gif* image. When you deselect it, it appears to blend into the background because its canvas is transparent. To emphasize the graphic, enter a 1 in the Border field and press Tab. A thin, 1-pixel wide border is displayed around the image, as shown in Figure 4.6. The color of the border is taken from the link color—blue by default. Try different Border values, such as 2, 5, and 10, to see the effect. To explicitly turn off the border, enter a 0 in the field.

Figure 4.6
Quickly add a frame around your image with the Border attribute.

Try It Yourself ▼

To understand how to use the margin controls better, follow these steps:

1. Open the file *shepherds_watch.htm* from this chapter's Media folder.

2. Select the first image of the ring.

3. In the H Space field of the Property inspector, enter a 5 and press Tab. Dreamweaver place a 5-pixel space on both the left and right side of the selected image, separating the text and graphic a bit. Because the margin is applied to both the left and right sides equally, you have to be careful not to use large values that would cause the image to stick out of the page too much.

4. Select the second image, the pendant.

5. In the V Space field, enter a 10 and press Tab. A 10-pixel space is to the top and bottom of the image, separating it from the text (see Figure 4.7). Experiment with different values to see the effect it has on the text.

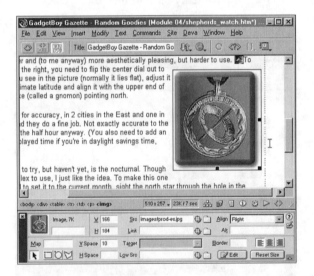

Figure 4.7
Give your image some breathing room with the Horizontal and Vertical margin properties.

6. Of course, you can have both horizontal and vertical margins; enter a 5 in the H space field of the second image to see that effect.

Building a Rollover

A *rollover*—somewhat similar to a hover button in FrontPage—takes place when the user's mouse passes over a graphic and the graphic changes in some way. It might appear to glow or change its shape, and then when the mouse moves away, the image returns to its original form.

There are several ways to create rollovers in Dreamweaver. Perhaps the simplest one is by using the Rollover Image object. To use this object, you'll need two separate images, which you can create in any image editor.

▼ **Try It Yourself**

1. To begin, drag the Insert Rollover Image button from the Common category of the Objects panel to any existing location on the Web page. Dreamweaver will open the Insert Rollover Image dialog box shown in Figure 4.8.

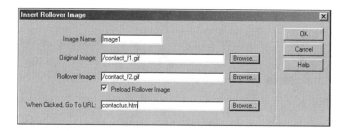

Figure 4.8
You'll need two similar, but separate, images before you can properly use the Insert Rollover Image command.

2. If desired, you can leave the name automatically generated by Dreamweaver or enter a unique name for the image in the Image Name text box.

3. Next to the Original Image text box, choose the Browse button to select the *contact_f1.gif* file found in this chapter's Media folder. This is the initial on-screen image. Press Tab when you're finished.

4. In the Rollover Image text box, enter the path and name of the graphic you want displayed when the user's pointer is over the graphic. In this example, we'll choose *contact_f2.gif*.

5. Specify a link for the image by entering it in the When Clicked, Go To URL text box. Clear the placeholding pound sign and enter *contact.htm*.

6. Be sure to leave the PreLoad option selected so that no delay occurs in the rollover appearing.

7. Click OK when you're finished.

Optimizing an Image with Fireworks

To strike the right balance of file size and image quality, most, if not all, images should be optimized for the Web. Optimizing could mean resizing, cropping, or reducing the number of colors or quality of an image. If you have Fireworks, you can optimize images in any of these ways right from within Dreamweaver.

Try It Yourself ▼

To use the Optimize Image in Fireworks command, follow these steps:

1. Open the file *optimize.htm* from the Media folder for this chapter.

2. In Dreamweaver, select the first image with the hand.

3. Resize the image by dragging the corner sizing handle and holding the Shift key. Remember, the Shift key keeps the dimensions the same.

   Make the image about 75% of its original size.

4. Choose Commands→Optimize Image in Fireworks.

5. If your Fireworks Preferences are set to ask whether a source file should be used in editing, the Find Source dialog box opens. In this case, choose No to work with the exported file. The Optimize Images dialog box appears.

Tip
You also can invoke the Optimize Image in Fireworks command from the context menu—just (Control) [Right] click on the image.

6. Because we've already resized the image in Dreamweaver, Fireworks knows how much to rescale it. Switch to the File tab, as shown in Figure 4.9, to see the percentage and dimensions.

ADDING IMAGES 63

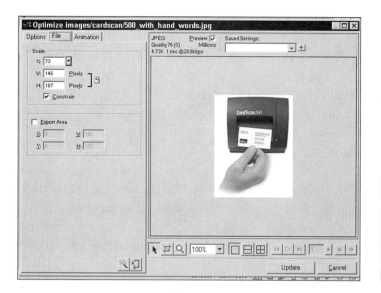

Figure 4.9
With the Optimize Image in Fireworks command, you can quickly scale or reduce the size of any graphic used in Dreamweaver.

7. If you're satisfied with that size, select the Update button.

You also can use the optimize command to change exported file types, reduce the number of colors, or crop the image. It's a real time saver.

Creating Layouts with Background Images

You can place as many foreground pictures as you'd like in Dreamweaver; however, you can use only one background image. As the name implies, a background image is viewed behind the text and graphics. Background images are used in many ways, including

- As a solid color, designed to be safe from browser variations
- As a tiled pattern, creating a design
- As a vertical or horizontal column, aimed at assisting the overall look and feel

The background image has several special characteristics. First, you insert it by choosing a file from the Page Properties dialog box, rather than visually placing it. Second, browsers automatically tile any image to fill the size of the browser window. This feature, in standard HTML, is outside your control, but it can be used to great advantage.

Try It Yourself ▼

▲

Let's look at a couple of background images:

1. Choose Modify→Page Properties to open the Page Properties dialog box.

2. Select the Background Image Browse button and select the file *bg01.gif* from this chapter's Media folder.

3. Click OK to see the background applied.

This file, *bg01.gif*, is a flat color with a very subtle texture, as can be seen in Figure 4.10. Although I could get this same non-Web safe color from the Background Color swatch, the texture would not be there. Resize the Document window a couple of times and you'll see that the texture seamlessly tiles to fill the area.

Figure 4.10
A simple block graphic can give your Web page a textured background.

Using the background image to produce columns is a widely used technique. Background columns use the tiling property of browsers to their advantage. A typical background column image is either very thin and very wide (such as 16 pixels high by 1000 pixels wide) or very thin and very tall (16 wide by 1000 tall). The extreme measurements are to prevent the image from repeating in most browser windows.

For a vertical example that appears to fade into the background, select Modify→Page Properties and choose *bg02.gif* for the background image and click OK. This tiled column background (see Figure 4.11) is based on a 23 pixel high by 1000 pixel wide GIF image. With layers or tables, you could easily create a navigation section on the left over the azure color and leave the white area for content.

Figure 4.11
The tiling property of browsers can be used to create a columned background.

Working with Image Maps

Image maps enable designers to assign links to hotspots on a graphic. The hotspots can be any shape—a rectangle, a circle, or a polygon—unlike a standard image, which is always rectangular. Among other things, this means that you could assign hotspots to interlocking areas on a map, such as one for each state in a U.S. map, and each hotspot could open a new Web page or trigger an interactive behavior.

You'll find the image map creation tools on the Property inspector for any selected image. They're very straightforward to use and great for rapid navigation development.

The following steps demonstrate the use of the hotspot drawing tools to outline each of the three different kinds of hotspots:

▼ **Try It Yourself**

1. On a new, saved page, insert the graphic *imagemap01.jpg* from this chapter's Media folder.

2. Before you begin drawing hotspots, enter a unique name for this image map in the field next to the label Map and above the three hotspot tools.

3. From the bottom left of the Property inspector, select the Rectangle tool.

4. Click and drag a rectangle over the slate area of the graphic.

   When you release your mouse button, a pale blue rectangle with control points at each corner is created, as you see in Figure 4.12. The Hotspot Property inspector now displays the map attributes.

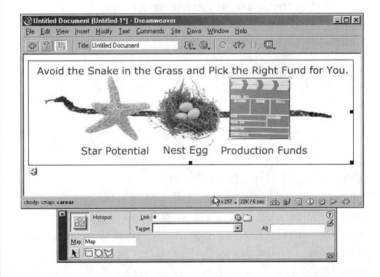

Figure 4.12
With Dreamweaver's rectangle Image Map tool, quickly drag out a hotspot and adjust its control points to refine the shape.

5. Enter the URL for this image map in the Link text box or click the folder icon and browse for the file.

6. If desired, enter a frame name or other target in the Target text box.

7. Enter any text you'd like to appear as a tool tip in the Alt text field.

If you need to adjust the placement of the hotspot or its shape, select the arrow tool and use it to move the entire hotspot or one of the control points.

Try It Yourself ▼

The next type of hotspot uses the Circle tool.

1. If you're still in the Hotspot Property Inspector, click anywhere outside the image, and then reselect the image.

2. Choose the Circle tool from the bottom of the Property inspector.

3. Starting at the upper-left corner, drag a circle around the nest portion of the graphic.

4. Complete the Link, Target, and Alt fields, if desired.

5. You can adjust the circle with the Pointer tool. Notice that dragging the control points only resizes the circle; you cannot turn it into an oval.

The final tool, the Polygon, is only slightly more difficult to use. The Polygon tool is used to define irregularly shaped hotspots.

▼ **Try It Yourself**

1. If you're still in the Hotspot Property Inspector, click anywhere outside the image, and then reselect the image.

2. Select the Polygon tool from the toolbar.

3. Click on one point of the starfish to start the hotspot.

   The goal with the Polygon tool is to completely outline the object. Although the hotspot might seem to be creating undesirable shapes, by the time the entire object is outlined, the hotspot will look like it's supposed to (see Figure 4.13).

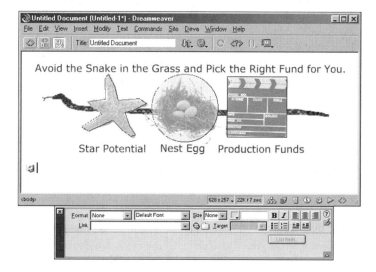

Figure 4.13
Dreamweaver includes rectangle, circle, and polygon Image Map tools.

4. Release the mouse button and move the mouse to the next point.

5. Continue outlining the object by clicking and moving the mouse.

6. When the hotspot is completely outlined, double-click the mouse to close the area.

7. To fully test this feature, fill in the Link, Target, and Alt text boxes.

Now if you test your image map in a browser, you'll see each hotspot leads to a different link.

Adding Flash Buttons

Although you primarily see Flash used in splash screens, interactive games, and standalone movies, it can be used for so much more. With Dreamweaver 4, you now can add Flash content to your Web pages directly from Dreamweaver—and you don't even need to know how to use Flash. Flash has been implemented in Dreamweaver in two exciting ways, through Flash buttons and Flash text (which we'll cover in the next section).

Try It Yourself ▼

With Flash buttons, you can easily create navigation bars that change when the user hovers their mouse over them, and you can even add audible feedback to your page by having your buttons play a sound when you click on them. To add Flash buttons, follow these simple steps:

1. If your document isn't saved, you need to save it. If you try to insert a Flash button into an unsaved document, Dreamweaver warns you about this.

2. Click on the Insert Flash Button object in the Common category of the Objects panel. The Flash Button dialog box is displayed, as shown in Figure 4.14.

3. Choose the button type you want from the Style box.

4. Type the text that you want to have displayed on your button.

5. Choose the desired font from the drop-down list and type the point size for your button text. Some Flash buttons are created with a specific font face and size to be used.

6. Next, you can type the URL for your button in the Link field or click on the Choose button to select a page from your site. If you are using frames, select from the Target drop-down list the appropriate frame into which the new page should load.

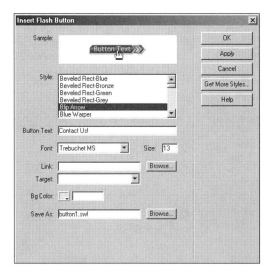

Figure 4.14
You don't even have to own Flash to make Flash Buttons from within Dreamweaver.

7. If the background color for the page that the button will be on is going to be anything other than white, set the Bg Color of your Flash button to match that color. This will improve the look of your button.

8. Finally, either name your button in the Save As Field or click Browse to navigate to where you want to save your new Flash button. If you want to see what your button looks like before closing the dialog box, click Apply and your button will be created and inserted into your document. Repeat these steps as necessary to create all the buttons you need for your design.

Dreamweaver ships with 44 different Flash button styles and even more are available from the Dreamweaver Exchange by clicking on the Get More Styles button. If you haven't used the Exchange, you'll find it discussed in a later chapter. Go ahead and make your own Flash buttons and then you can move on to Flash text!

Including Flash Text

One of the challenges faced by Web designers is how to create distinctive pages that look good and are easy to read and navigate. Given the limited font choices, it's often difficult to achieve just the right look for a site or, more importantly, a company logo. Here's where you see the power, and the beauty, of Flash text.

With Flash text, you can use any TrueType font on your system to create great-looking headings that have small file sizes but can be scaled without the worry of jagged edges. As with Flash buttons, everything can be created from within Dreamweaver with no complicated program to learn.

Try It Yourself ▼

To create some Flash text of your own, follow these steps:

1. Save your document from the last example, and then click on the Insert Flash Text icon in the Common category of the Objects panel.

2. In the Insert Flash Text dialog box (see Figure 4.15), choose the font face and size you want to use.

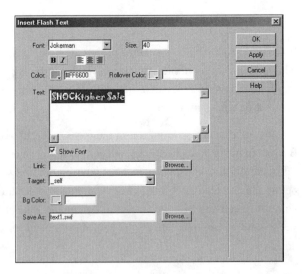

Figure 4.15
Flash Text can use any font on your system to create clear, sharp text— with or without a rollover!

3. You can choose to make your Flash text bold or italic, and even control whether the text you type will be aligned left, right, or centered.

4. Next, you can choose the color swatch in which you want your text displayed, or you can enter its hexadecimal value in the text field next to the Color box.

5. If you are going to use your Flash text as a link, you can even specify a Rollover Color so that the color of your text will change when the viewer's mouse is over it.

6. Now you can type your text in the Text field. Dreamweaver displays your text in the actual font you chose earlier so that you can see exactly how your Flash text will turn out. If you don't want to see this preview, simply deselect the Show Font check box.

7. If you're using your Flash text as a link, enter the URL in the Link field or click Browse to select the file. If you're using frames for your link, be sure to choose from the Target drop-down list the frame into which your page should open.

8. You should change the color in the Bg Color box if the background color of your document will be anything other than Dreamweaver's default of white. This just sets your Flash text's background to match that of your document, giving you a cleaner look.

9. Finally, you can enter a name for your Flash text right in the Save As box, or by clicking Browse and navigating to where you want to save it. If you click Apply, Dreamweaver will insert your Flash text into your document, and you can make any necessary tweaks without having to reopen the Insert Flash Text dialog box.

CHAPTER 5

Creating Links

Understanding Links

Links can be thought of as a postal address—often a very detailed address, but an address nonetheless. Links are also called URLs (or Uniform Resource Locators). Every item stored on a Web server accessible to the Internet can be reached by entering its address or link in the browser. When an item is no longer at its specified location, the link is said to be broken.

In this chapter, we'll look at links from one page to another, links within a page—called bookmarks in FrontPage, but known as *named anchors* in HTML—and e-mail links.

Applying Absolute and Relative Links

There are two basic types of links: absolute and relative. To continue the address metaphor, consider an *absolute link* to be like that found on a mailing label, but instead of name, street, city, state, and postal code, you have a domain name, folder and a Web page's filename. A *relative link* is similar to directions: "Oh, the Smiths? They're two doors down on the left. Can't miss 'em." Many Web sites use relative links to connect the pages within a site to one another and absolute links to connect to other sites. Dreamweaver handles both types of URLs through the Link field on the Property inspector.

Creating a basic link in Dreamweaver is very straightforward; rather than going through a separate dialog box as in FrontPage, links are assigned in the versatile Dreamweaver Property inspector. Just follow these steps:

1. Select the text, image, or object you want to establish as a link.

What You'll Learn in This Chapter:
- ▶ All about the different types of links
- ▶ How to use the Point-to-File icon
- ▶ How to create an e-mail link
- ▶ How to work with named anchors

▼ **Try It Yourself**

2. In the Property inspector, enter the URL in the Link text box, shown in Figure 5.1. You can either

    - Type the URL directly into the Link text box.
    - Select the folder icon next to the Link text box to open the Select HTML File dialog box, where you can locate the file.
    - Use the Point-to-File icon (covered in the next section).

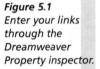

Figure 5.1
Enter your links through the Dreamweaver Property inspector.

Whenever possible, I avoid typing the address and use the second or third methods given above. Not only does this prevent typos, but you'll also get the proper path automatically added in Dreamweaver.

Pointing to a File

Try It Yourself ▼

The Point-to-File feature is intended for relative links. To use this feature, you'll need to have your screen set up so that you can see both the Document window and the Site window side by side.

1. As before, select the text or image to which you want to create a link.

2. Now, select the Point-to-File icon and drag your mouse to an existing page or link on the Site window, as seen in Figure 5.2.

Creating Links

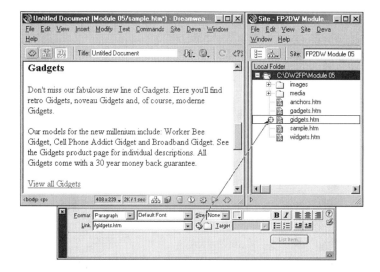

Figure 5.2
The Point-to-File method is a great way to link to files in your site quickly.

3. If the link you want is in an unopened folder, just pass the Point-to-File icon over the folder and it will open.

4. After you've selected a file, release your mouse and the proper filename appears in the Link text field.

Creating an E-Mail Link

You see *e-mail links*, or "mailto" links, everywhere on the Web. Unlike a regular link that opens a new Web page, when an e-mail link is clicked, a window for sending a new e-mail message appears in your default e-mail client. Conveniently, the new message window is preaddressed to the recipient. The user only needs to add a subject and message, and then select Send.

E-mail links normally would need to be added by hand, but Dreamweaver includes an object that'll do the work for you. Just enter the text for the link and the e-mail address, and the link is ready.

To enter an e-mail link with the new object, follow these steps:

▼ **Try It Yourself**

1. Position your cursor where you want the e-mail link to appear.

2. From the Common category of the Objects panel, select the Insert Email Link button.

Figure 5.3
Enter the text and e-mail address in one action with the Insert Email Link dialog box.

3. In the Insert Email Link dialog box (see Figure 5.3), enter the visible text for the link in the Text field.

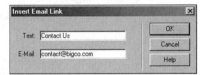

4. Enter the e-mail address in the Email field. The e-mail address must be in the format *name@company.com*. Dreamweaver does not check to make sure you've entered the proper format.

5. Click OK when you're finished.

E-mail links, like other links, do not work in Dreamweaver when clicked and must be previewed in the browser.

If you already have the text or a graphic for the e-mail link in the document, you can also use the Property inspector to insert an e-mail link. Just highlight the text in the Link field of the Property inspector and enter the URL in this format:

mailto:name@company.com

Be sure that the URL is a valid e-mail address with the @ sign properly placed.

Note
Your mailto link can even set the subject for your e-mail with a little extra coding. After the *mailto:* address, add a question mark followed by the word *subject*, an equal sign, and the subject itself, like this:

mailto:sales@bigco.com?subject=Sales-Arama

Your subject cannot contain any regular spaces; if you need to include a space, it must be represented by %20. Here's another example that sets the subject to "Big Sales Event":

mailto:sales@bigco.com?subject=Big%20Sales%20Event

Working with Anchors

Loading a page in your browser with a standard link always causes the page to display from the top. It's possible, however, to connect to any other point on the page, instantly zooming to a specific section. To do this, you need to use a special type of link called a *named anchor*—in FrontPage it's called a *bookmark*.

Using named anchors is basically a two-step process. First, you place a named anchor somewhere on your Web page. The second step is to create a link to that named anchor from somewhere else on your Web page or another page. Links to named anchors are instantly recognizable by the initial hash mark (#).

CREATING LINKS 77

Let's step through the process for creating a named anchor:

▼ **Try It Yourself**

1. Open the *named_anchor.htm* file in Dreamweaver, found in the Media folder for this chapter.

2. Place your cursor next to the third study on the page, "Rethinking the PPM Industry."

3. Choose Insert→Named Anchor. You also can select the Insert Named Anchor button from the Invisibles category of the Objects panel.

Note

As with other invisible symbols, the Named Anchor symbol can be cut and pasted or moved using the drag-and-drop method. Sometimes after testing you'll find that you need to move the anchor a bit to make the browser go where you want it to.

4. The Named Anchor dialog box opens. Type the anchor name into the text box. Named anchors are case sensitive and must be unique. I try to enter logical names; here, I'd either use *rethinking* or *ppm* as a name.

5. When you press Enter, Dreamweaver places a Named Anchor symbol in the current cursor location and opens the Named Anchor Property inspector, as seen in Figure 5.4. Now that the anchor is placed, let's link to it.

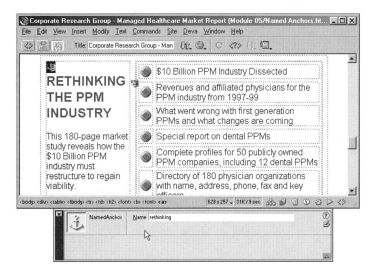

Figure 5.4
Named anchors are great for navigating around a long page.

6. Select the text or image that you want to designate as a link. In this case, it's the "Rethinking the PPM Industry" graphic slice near the top of the page.

7. In the Link text box of the Property inspector, type a hash mark, #, followed by the exact anchor name. For example, *#rethinking*.

8. Press F12 to preview the page in a browser and test your named anchors.

You also can use the Point-to-File icon to insert the link. Click and drag the Point-to-File icon down the page (Dreamweaver will scroll automatically) to point to the named anchor. When you release the mouse, the named anchor link is inserted.

CHAPTER 6

Using Layout View

Introducing Layout View

The new Layout View in Dreamweaver 4 greatly simplifies the creation of tables by allowing you to draw your tables and cells right in the document window. In Layout view, you can easily set tables to automatically stretch to fit the size of the browser window.

Inserting a Tracing Image

Although you certainly can use Layout view without a tracing image, it's a little easier to understand when you do. A *tracing image* is a graphic used during design time to ensure that the proper layout is followed. Tracing images do not appear in the browser window, only in Dreamweaver.

1. To insert a tracing image, choose Modify→Page Properties.

2. Near the bottom of the dialog box, choose the Browse button next to the Tracing Image field, as shown in Figure 6.1. Locate the file *tracingimage.png* in the Media folder for this chapter.

   You can alter the opacity of the tracing image by moving the Transparency slider, but for this demonstration leave it at 100%.

What You'll Learn in This Chapter:
- Why Layout view is so useful
- What a tracing image is and how to use it
- How to work with tables in Dreamweaver

▼ **Try It Yourself**

Figure 6.1
Tracing Images are inserted through the Page Properties dialog box.

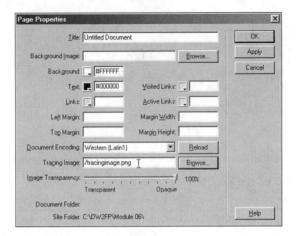

3. Click OK when you're finished.

When you return to the Document window, you'll notice your tracing image is in place. To verify that this is only for design-time work, select F12 to see the page in a browser. Come back to Dreamweaver and you're ready to move into Layout View.

Using Layout View for Quick Design

Try It Yourself ▼

Switching in and out of Layout view couldn't be easier because the buttons are located right at the bottom of the Objects panel. To enter Layout view, simply click the Layout view button, shown in Figure 6.2. If you want to leave Layout view, it's just a matter of clicking the Standard view button. You can use Layout view to modify existing tables but it really shines when you are starting a page from scratch, or as in this case, using a tracing image.

1. Click the Layout view button. When you enter Layout view, Dreamweaver displays a dialog box that explains how Layout view works. It's probably a good idea to leave your settings alone for a while so that this screen continues to get displayed, but when you're familiar with Layout view, you can turn it off by clicking the Don't Show Me This Message Again check box.

2. Click the Draw Layout Cell button (on the left, just above the view mode buttons) and your cursor will become a plus sign.

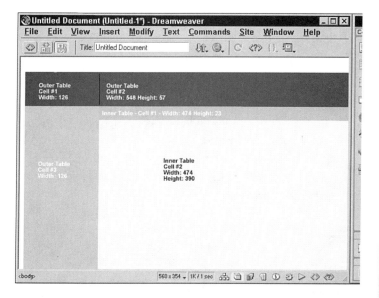

Figure 6.2
Switch in and out of Layout view by using the icons at the bottom of the Objects panel.

3. Click and drag in the document window to trace out your first cell. Let's do the one in the upper-left corner of our tracing image, Outer Table Cell #1. When you release the mouse button, Dreamweaver creates the table and your table cell, as shown in Figure 6.3. It might seem strange to draw out the cell first rather than create the table first, but as you'll see next, it's best to use the Draw Layout Table command for nested tables.

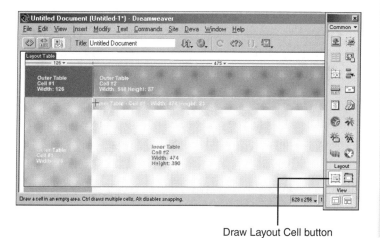

Draw Layout Cell button

Figure 6.3
When you draw your first cell in Layout view, Dreamweaver constructs the remainder of the table automatically.

4. Now that you've got your first cell, repeat the same steps to draw out the rest of the Outer Table cells. Don't worry if you don't get it exactly on the tracing image, you can easily fine-tune the layout later.

5. After you've finished drawing out the other two outer cells, click the Draw Layout Cell button again to deselect it. Now your cursor is a pointer and you can manipulate the tables and cells. Click on the outer border of the table and drag the sizing handle on the right side until it matches the tracing image, as shown in Figure 6.4.

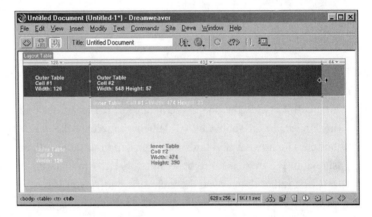

Figure 6.4
Once selected, you can adjust the placement, size, and shape of any layout cell.

Tip
When you finish drawing out each cell, Dreamweaver switches the cursor back to the standard I-beam so that you're ready to insert assets into your new cell. Instead of having to click the Draw Layout Cell button for each new cell, you can hold down the Ctrl (Command) button while dragging your first cell to tell Dreamweaver that you want to continue drawing more cells.

Try It Yourself ▼

6. Adjust any of the other cells to match. You'll notice that the borders of the cell turn red when they can be selected. You can also (Command-click) [Ctrl+click] in any cell to select it. Once selected, the sizing handles appear and you adjust the dimensions.

Nesting Tables

As mentioned before, you use the Draw Layout Table command to create nested tables. To create a nested table in Layout View, follow these steps:

1. If you aren't there already, get into Layout View by selecting its button from the Objects panel.

2. Click on the Draw Layout Table button from the Objects panel.

3. When your cursor is over the portion of a table with no cells, it will become a plus sign. Click and drag to draw out a nested table over the open rectangle, as shown in Figure 6.5.

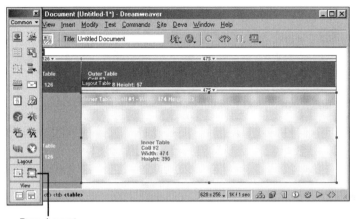

Figure 6.5
The Draw Layout Table command allows you to easily create nested tables.

Draw Layout Table button

4. To add cells to your nested table, simply select the Draw Layout Cell button and draw out the two inner table cells like you did with the outer table cells.

5. After you've set up your inner and outer tables to match the tracing image, turn off the tracing image so you can see the results. Choose View→Tracing Image→Show and you'll see that it's currently checked; choosing it again will turn it off.

Modifying Cell Properties

Tables and cells, when in Layout View, have their own Property inspector. Although it's similar to the ones seen in standard view, there are a few key differences. First, let's show you how to invoke the right Property inspector:

▼ **Try It Yourself**

1. Click in Cell #1 of the outer table in the upper-left. You'll notice that the Property inspector is the standard text inspector without any table- or cell-specific attributes.

2. Now, Ctrl+click (Command-click on the Mac) into the same cell. The Property inspector changes, showing the attributes of the Layout Cell as seen in Figure 6.6.

Figure 6.6
The Layout Cell Property inspector gives quick access to a cell's most commonly used attributes.

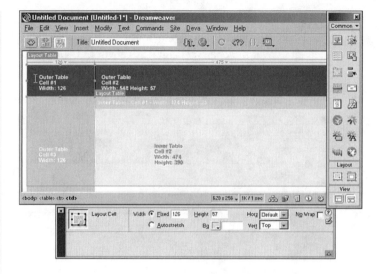

3. Let's change the background color of our cells to match the tracing image. Select the Bg color swatch to bring up the color picker.

4. Use the eyedropper to sample the bluish gray color in the tracing image's cell.

5. Follow the same procedure for each cell where there is a color—[Ctrl+click] (Command-click), select the color swatch, sample the background—until you're finished.

You might have noticed the term Autostretch in the Property inspectors—I'll explain what that means next.

Working with Autostretch

At this point, all the cells and columns in our table are fixed—that is, they are a specific pixel width and will not get any wider regardless of the amount of text we use: The table will only grow in height. The cells will get wider to accommodate a larger image, however. Although a fixed layout is good for some situations, when the page is viewed through a browser with a higher resolution—anything larger than 640×480, in fact—an amount of white space will appear to the right of the table. Many designers, including myself, prefer to create layouts that stretch to fit the size of the user's screen.

For this purpose, Dreamweaver includes an Autostretch feature. Autostretch does two things. First, it changes the width of a column from a fixed pixel size to a percentage—100%, in fact. Now, whenever the browser window changes size, the table column changes size with it. The second thing Autostretch does is add an additional 1 pixel-high row on the bottom of a table containing a 1 pixel-high transparent GIF image, called a spacer. This GIF is added to every other column except the one set to 100%; it serves to lock the table into its designed shape. Without the spacer, the table would break apart in certain browsers. Let's see how it works:

▼ **Try It Yourself**

1. Switch to Layout View, if not already there.

2. Choose the width indicator above Cell #2 of the Outer Table.

3. From the drop-down menu choose Make Column Autostretch. The Choose Spacer Image dialog box will appear, as shown in Figure 6.7.

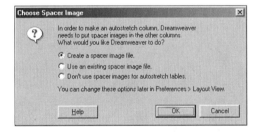

Figure 6.7
Dreamweaver enables you to set the type of spacer you want to use for each site.

4. This dialog box gives you several options for creating the spacer image. Let's let Dreamweaver do the work for us by selecting Create a Spacer Image File. Click OK.

5. Dreamweaver then asks you where you want to store the spacer image in your site. For now, let's leave it in the site root—click Save to continue.

6. Dreamweaver automatically adds all the necessary spacers, which in this example is just one. To see it, click the table border to select the entire table.

7. Now, go into Split Code and Design View.

Try It Yourself

8. Scroll down the code window to the end of the highlighted table section. You should see one line of code that looks something like this:

    ```
    <td height="1"><img height="1" width="126" src="/spacer.gif"></td>
    ```

9. Return to Design view and let's test our Autostretching table by choosing F12 to preview the page in the browser.

10. Resize the browser window back and forth. You should see that while the right column changes width, the first column—where the spacer is—remains constant.

You might notice a white margin around the table. This is the normal margin on an HTML page. To remove the margins, choose Modify→Page Properties again and enter a 0 (zero) in each of the four Margin settings (Left Margin, Top Margin, Margin Width, and Margin Height).

CHAPTER 7

Previewing Your Page

Web Page Testing

As with FrontPage, Dreamweaver's design window only approximates how a Web page eventually is to be viewed. Both programs offer a Preview in Browser feature for seeing the page in progress as the user will see it. FrontPage, however, enables you to view your page in only one browser. Dreamweaver takes a more real-world approach and enables you to review your pages in any number of browsers. In Dreamweaver, you can define both a primary and a secondary browser—available with the press of a keyboard shortcut—as well access up to a dozen additional browsers, if they're installed on your system.

In a business where changes happen on Internet time, Dreamweaver's multifaceted Preview in Browser feature is essential.

Using Preview in Browser

If you've been following along in the previous chapters, you've already encountered Dreamweaver's Preview in Browser feature. Instead of a Preview tab like the one found in FrontPage, Dreamweaver previews by launching a new browser window, as shown in Figure 7.1. The browser loads a temporary file, which actually is a saved copy of your page, to allow you complete testing. These temporary files are deleted from your system when you quit your Dreamweaver session.

What You'll Learn in This Chapter:
- ▶ How to test your page in a browser
- ▶ How to set up multiple browsers for testing
- ▶ How to use browser profiles

Figure 7.1
With Dreamweaver's Preview in Browser system, you can see the layout and browser views at the same time; here, the Dreamweaver representation is on top and the browser view is beneath it.

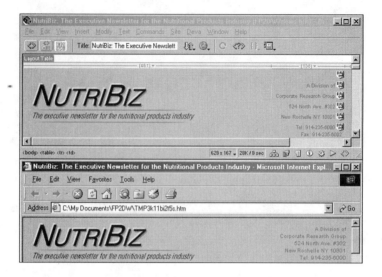

There are a number of ways to preview a current page in Dreamweaver; perhaps the fastest way is to press F12. This launches what is called your *primary browser*. If you haven't defined a primary browser in Dreamweaver—as we'll do later in this lesson—Dreamweaver uses your system browser initially.

Besides using the function key, F12, to preview a page, you also can

- Choose File→Preview in Browser and then select the desired browser from the drop-down list.

- From the Toolbar, click the Preview/Debug in Browser button, the globe symbol, and select the browser.

- If you're working in the Dreamweaver's Site window, you can select a file and then choose File→Preview in Browser or (Ctrl) [Right] click and use the context menu option.

To gain the most benefit from the Preview in Browser feature, you need to set up additional browsers for testing—you'll see how that's done in the next section.

Setting Up Multiple Browsers

At the very least, I recommend that—unless you're working in an intranet environment where you are creating pages for only one browser—you define at least two browsers to act as your primary and secondary browser. Currently, I have Internet Explorer 5.5 listed as my primary browser and Netscape 6 as my secondary browser; in addition, I am set up so I can check my pages against Netscape 4.7.

Let's step through the process of defining a primary browser first:

▼ **Try It Yourself**

1. From the Toolbar, choose the Preview in Browser button and select Edit Browser List from the menu. This command will take you right to the Preview in Browser category of Preferences, shown in Figure 7.2.

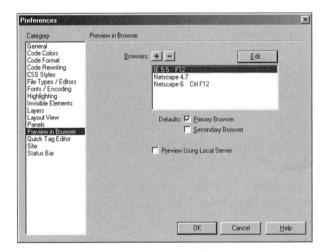

Figure 7.2
Set up alternative browsers through Dreamweaver's Preferences.

2. Click the Add (+) button to open up the Add Browser dialog box.

3. Click the Browse button to pick the file from the Select Browser dialog box. (Don't enter the name first, because Dreamweaver will overwrite it anyway.) Navigate to the executable for your browser application and choose Open.

4. After you have selected your browser application, Dreamweaver fills in the Name field. You can alter this name if you want—the name in this field appears in all the menu lists, so make it something brief and meaningful.

5. Designate this browser as your Primary browser by selecting that check box in the Defaults section.

6. Click OK when you have finished to close the Add Browser button.

If you're ready to add more browsers, repeat all these steps except the final one where you selected the Primary option. You can actually add a dozen more browsers, if you like.

After you've added a browser to your list, you can change its name by selecting it from the list and then choosing Edit. You also can remove browsers in the list by selecting the Remove button, the minus symbol. Finally, to alter your Primary or Secondary choices, just select the browser you want as Primary and check that option; the same thing is true for your Secondary browser.

By the way, unless you're working with dynamic pages such as Active Server Pages, you'll probably want to leave the Preview Using Local Server option unchecked.

Note
If you're working from a page in progress, you should save it before you check it. If you don't, Dreamweaver will prompt you that it only checks the saved version of the page, not the one in memory, and will give you the choice of saving it.

Checking Your Page Against Browser Profiles

Viewing your page in another browser on your system is great, but what if you don't have all the browsers installed that you need to check? Dreamweaver provides a tool for checking your page's code against a wide variety of past and current browsers called Browser Profiles. With the Browser Profiles, you can effectively target specific browsers and test them a page at a time or run the entire site all at once.

Try It Yourself ▼

Let's compare a page against some Browser Profiles to see how it works.

1. From the Media folder for this chapter, open *news.htm*.

2. Select File→Check Target Browsers to open the dialog box shown in Figure 7.3.

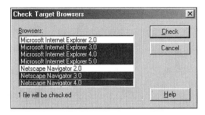

Figure 7.3
With the Check Target Browser features you can check your page for errors against browsers you don't even have on your system.

3. Choose the browsers against which you want to check the page. For multiple selections, hold down the (Command) [Ctrl] key while making your selections, or hold down the Shift key for a contiguous selection.

   In this example, don't worry about the 2.0 browsers, but select every other available browser.

4. When you're ready, select Check. The primary browser is opened and a report appears, as shown in Figure 7.4.

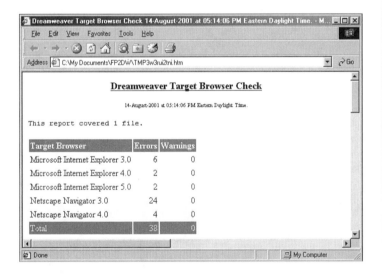

Figure 7.4
The results from a Check Target Browser report appear in the browser window.

5. Looking over the report, you'll find a summary of the errors as well as a detail section. If you find an error you can't live with, you can go back to the page and find the error on its given line number.

   In this particular report, my biggest concern is the large number of errors occurring in Netscape 3.0 browsers. Upon closer examination, I see that most of the problems stem from the

Class and Span tags not being supported. I know that these are Cascading Style Sheet tags, so, if I wanted, I could go back into my page and add additional HTML formatting to make sure that the pages would look right in all browsers.

You should know that Dreamweaver saves the report only temporarily and removes it after its use. If you need to maintain a record of the report, you can use your browser's File→Print or File→Save command.

If you wanted to check more than one page, select the files desired in the Site window before you choose File→Check Target Browser. Select the very uppermost folder in the Site files pane to check the entire site.

Dreamweaver will tell you how many files will be checked. The report lists the errors for each file separately in the Detail section. Dreamweaver even provides you with a series of links to each file so you quickly can check the errors on the most important files.

CHAPTER 8

Adding Interactivity

Understanding Behaviors

So, you've mastered HTML's tags syntax, conquered Dynamic HTML layout with layers and CSS, and now someone tells you that if you want to make your page interactive, you have to learn JavaScript!?! Although it's true that almost every effect you see on standard Web pages is accomplished through a combination of HTML and JavaScript, with Dreamweaver, you don't have to master another computer language—Dreamweaver does it for you.

A Dreamweaver *behavior* is made up of two essential, interconnected parts: the event and the action. The *event* is the trigger and can be anything: a mouse click, moving the cursor over an area, or even having a page completely load. The *action* is what happens: a new browser window opens, a message appears in the status bar, a layer moves dynamically across the screen, and so on. Behaviors are somewhat like FrontPage's Dynamic HTML effects, but with much greater flexibility.

There are three basic steps to adding a Dreamweaver behavior to a page:

1. **Select a page element**—Behaviors are triggered by an interaction with a particular page element, and only certain types of elements are eligible. Generally, a link (either text or image) or the <body> tag is used. Links do not have to be active—that is, they do not have to open a new page—you can use so-called false links, either an unspecified named anchor *(#)* or a JavaScript function call.

2. **Choose the behavior**—You can choose any available behavior from the drop-down list on the Behaviors panel. Whether a behavior is available depends on the behavior itself. Certain

What You'll Learn in This Chapter:
- What behaviors have to do with interactivity in Dreamweaver
- How to attach and edit a behavior

ones require specific elements (a layer or an image, for example) to be present or selected. If the condition is not met, the behavior is shown as being inactive.

3. **Select the parameters**—Most (although not all) behaviors include a custom dialog box to allow user-selectable options. These attributes can be adjusted at any time by double-clicking the behavior in the Behaviors panel.

Attaching a Simple Behavior

Try It Yourself ▼

Let's start with a simple behavior example, the pop-up message:

1. Create and save a new page.

2. Type a single word, and then select it and make it a link by entering a hash mark, #, in the Link field of the Property inspector.

3. Choose Window→Behaviors to open the Behaviors panel, shown in Figure 8.1.

Figure 8.1
The Behaviors panel is "interaction central" in Dreamweaver.

4. Select the Add Behavior button (the plus sign) and choose Popup Message from the list. The Popup Message dialog box appears.

Note

The length of your longest line sets the width of the pop-up message box. You can use paragraph returns in the Popup Message dialog box to shape how your text appears on screen.

5. Enter a line or two you want to appear in the Message field. Click OK when you're finished.

6. You'll notice a single line has been added to the Behaviors panel that lists the triggering Event on the left (*onClick*) and the resulting Action (*PopupMessage*) on the right, as shown in Figure 8.2.

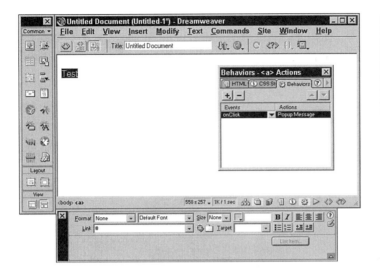

Figure 8.2
Each behavior is listed on its own line and shows the Event and its corresponding Action.

7. Test your new behavior by pressing F12, Preview in Browser, and then clicking on the link.

Your message should appear instantly in an alert box. The wording that appears in the title bar ("Microsoft Internet Explorer" in Internet Explorer and "[JavaScript Application]" in Navigator) cannot be altered.

Changing a Behavior's Event

Although it seems perfectly natural to click on a link and get a pop-up message as we did in the last lesson, what if you wanted the same behavior to be triggered by a mouse-over instead? Dreamweaver automatically inserts a particular event based on the tag to which the behavior is being applied, and the category of behavior selected. However, you can easily change the event from a drop-down list on the Behaviors panel.

Let's change our existing event trigger from a mouse-click to a mouse-over:

▼ **Try It Yourself**

1. Continue with the file used in the last example.

2. Place your cursor in the text that triggered the behavior.

3. In the Behaviors panel, select the previously attached behavior.

Figure 8.3
The Events For submenu is an important part of attaching Dreamweaver behaviors.

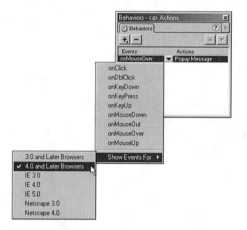

4. Click the down arrow in the behavior to see the available events. Go all the way to the bottom to be sure the Events For menu is pointing to the 4.0 Browsers and Later option (see Figure 8.3); if not, select it.

5. Choose *onMouseOver* from the Event list.

6. Preview your page in a browser to see the change; now your message is displayed when the user's mouse moves over the link, instead of when clicking on it.

With the later browsers, especially Internet Explorer 5.x, you can trigger actions with many more kinds of events. To see what I mean, change the Events For option on the Behaviors panel to IE 5.0, and then select the down triangle to see the Event list. The nine events available to both 4.0+ browsers are expanded to a mind-blowing 31 with Internet Explorer 5.0 selections.

Modifying Inserted Behaviors

After you've attached your behavior to a tag, nothing about it is set in stone. Any or all parameters can be altered or, if desired, the entire behavior can be removed. Just select the unwanted behavior in the panel and click the Remove button. When you delete a behavior, Dreamweaver removes all the accompanying code.

Try It Yourself ▼

Instead of modifying our simple Popup Message behavior, let's look at a slightly more complex and very useful example, Open Browser Window:

ADDING INTERACTIVITY

1. Open the file *behavior_ex.htm* from this chapter's Media folder.

   In this file, a couple of behaviors have already been attached to the image. Select the image and, in the Behaviors panel, you'll see two Show/Hide Layers behaviors with two different events. As you might suspect, a layer is displayed *onMouseOver* and hidden *onMouseOut*. Preview the file in a browser to see exactly what happens. As the layer indicates, clicking on the image will display the full screen—and that's the behavior we're going to add and modify.

2. Select the image and, in the Behaviors panel, choose Open Browser Window from the Add Behavior list. The Open Browser Window dialog box is displayed, as seen in Figure 8.4.

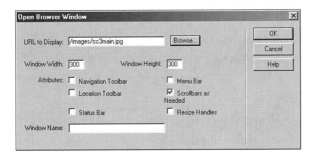

Figure 8.4
Each behavior has its own dialog box, like this one for the Open Browser Window behavior.

3. In the URL to Display field, use the Browse button to locate the *cc3main.jpg* file in the Media/images folder.

   Now let's limit the size of the new browser window opening so that both the review and the image can be on the same screen.

4. Set the Width and Height values to 300 each.

5. Under Attributes, select only the Scrollbars as Needed option. Click OK when you're finished.

6. Preview your page to see the effect, moving over the image to see the layer appear, and then click on the image to see the new window, as shown in Figure 8.5.

Note
The name option is used only when you want to further control your window with JavaScript.

Figure 8.5
Dreamweaver behaviors give you the power to add complex interactions without knowing JavaScript.

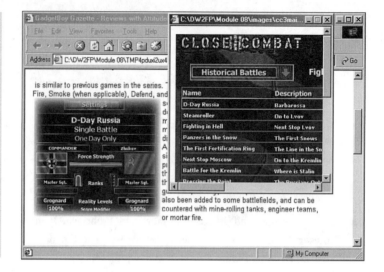

Try It Yourself

Let's say that after previewing it, we decide to alter the size to make it more horizontal.

1. In Dreamweaver, select the image from the Behaviors panel and double-click the Open Browser Window behavior. The dialog box reappears, with all of your attributes set appropriately.

2. Change the Width value to 400 and the Height to 200. Click OK when you're finished.

3. Continue previewing and modifying your behavior until it looks the way you want.

As you've probably noticed when looking through the Behavior list, there are a lot of options with the standard Dreamweaver behaviors. In Chapter 12, "Extending Dreamweaver," you'll see how to add custom behaviors to perform almost any action you could want.

CHAPTER 9

Including Library Items

Why Use Libraries?

Many elements on a Web page—a corporate logo, a copyright notice, a navigation bar—are the same on many pages in a given Web site. When you need to update those elements, you often have to go through every page to make the change. Not, however, if your element is a Dreamweaver Library item. With Library items, you can change one element, and all the other pages which use that element are automatically updated.

Library elements are a great way to boost your productivity. You'll also find them useful if you're co-developing a site and want to share your resources with other team members.

What You'll Learn in This Chapter:
- What a Library is used for in Dreamweaver
- How to create and modify Library items
- How to update Library items by Web page or for an entire site

Creating Library Items

Almost anything you can see on a Web page can be turned into a Library item: text, graphics, media files, and ActiveX controls, to name a few.

Library items are specific to each site and are managed—created, inserted, modified, and deleted—through the Assets panel. After they're created, all Library items are stored in a special folder, craftily called Library, which Dreamweaver creates for you. The Library folder resides on your local site and doesn't need to be uploaded to the remote site.

Note
About the only things that can't be turned into a Library item are elements found in the head section of a Web page, such as meta tags. However, there are extensions available for Dreamweaver that can automate managing meta tags.

Let's start by taking a simple example—in this case, a copyright line—create a Library item, and then use it.

▼ **Try It Yourself**

1. Open the page *products.htm* from the Media folder for this chapter.

2. Scroll down to the bottom of the page and type the line *Copyright © 2001 NutriBiz*—remember, you can use the

Characters category of the Objects panel to create the copyright symbol (c-in-circle).

3. Choose Window→Library to open the Library category of the Assets panel.

   You also could click the Assets panel button on the Launcher and then click the Library button.

4. Select the copyright line and drag-and-drop it into either pane of the Assets panel, top or bottom.

   When you drop the text, you'll see the rendered code appear in the upper preview pane and a new Untitled item appears in the lower list.

5. Change Untitled to something like "copyright." You might notice in the listed path that the item is stored in the Library folder with an *.lbi* extension, shown in Figure 9.1.

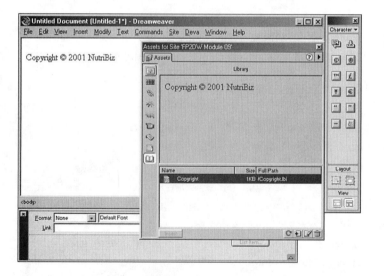

Figure 9.1
Library items are stored in the Assets panel and are instantly available.

Now, click back on your page onto the copyright line. If you have your Property inspector open, you'll see that it is now a Library item, not just a text block. Click anywhere to deselect the item, and you should see the text highlighted in yellow. If you don't see the highlight, choose the View Options button on the Toolbar and select Visual Aids→Invisible Elements to enable the highlighting.

Including Library Items

Now, with a Library item defined, let's see how easy it is to add them to a page.

Inserting Library Items into a Page

It's time to open another page and begin using our previously defined Library item:

▼ **Try It Yourself**

1. Open *order.htm* from the Media folder for the current chapter.

2. Scroll to the bottom of the page and drag the copyright library item from the Assets panel onto the page. You can drag the Library item from either the top or the bottom panes of the panel.

3. The copyright line will appear instantly, as shown in Figure 9.2.

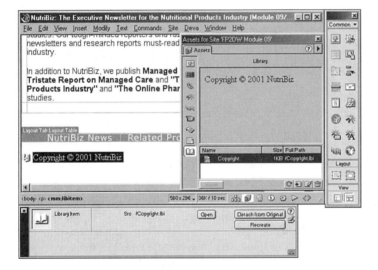

Figure 9.2
Use Library items on as many pages as you like.

Tip

For more complex layouts, you also can position your cursor where you'd like the Library item to appear, select it in the Assets panel, and then choose Insert.

▲

Modifying Library Items

Quickly inserting commonly used elements, such as the copyright line, is roughly half the magic of Dreamweaver Library items. To understand the other primary feature of Library items, all we have to do is modify one.

▼ **Try It Yourself**

1. From any page in your site—whether it has the Library item included or not—open the Library section of the Assets panel.

2. Double-click on the copyright item in the Library category of the Assets panel to begin editing it.

   Editing a Library item launches a new Dreamweaver window. At the top of the window you should see the phrase "Library Item" surrounded by double angle brackets, as shown in Figure 9.3.

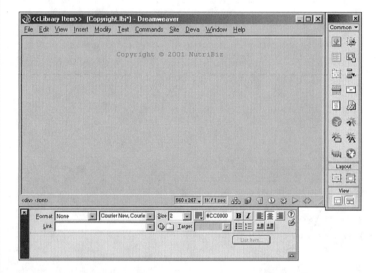

Figure 9.3
Modifying a Library item is handled in a new Dreamweaver window.

3. Select the text and change its format with the Property inspector. First, center it, and then change the font to Courier New, Courier. Next, reduce it in size by choosing Size 2. Finally, color it so it's less noticeable on a page by choosing a medium gray from the color picker.

4. When you're finished, choose File→Save to store the changes and begin the update process.

5. In the Update Library Items dialog box that appears, you'll see all the files in which the Library item has been inserted. Click Update to apply the changes you made to all the files.

6. Dreamweaver shows its progress in the Update Pages dialog box. When it's finished, select Close.

Now, check your pages containing the Library item. You'll notice that all the changes applied are found on both instances.

If you want, you can defer the updates to a later time. Generally, the only reason you would do this is if you have to change several Library items and you'd like to run them all at once. Details on how to do this are in the next section.

Updating Library Items on Web Pages

Whether you need to update the Library items on just the current page or throughout the site, Dreamweaver has got you covered.

Choose Modify→Library→Update Current Page to update just the current page.

Updating an entire Web site is a little more involved, but not terribly difficult. To get a truer picture of how it works, you'll need to define at least one other Library item. For the purposes of this demo, select the NutriBiz logo, found on *order.htm*, and drag it into the Library category of the Assets panel. Give it a name and you're ready to go.

1. Select Modify→Library→Update Pages to open the dialog box (see Figure 9.4).

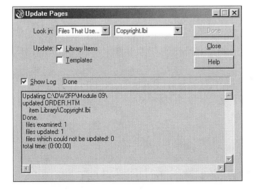

Figure 9.4
The Update Pages dialog box shows all the pages containing the current item.

2. To update all the Library items in all the Web pages in your site, select Entire Site from the Look In drop-down list, and choose the name of your site in the drop-down list on the right.

   As you can see, not only can you modify the Library items in your current site, but also those contained in any site.

3. You can limit Dreamweaver to updating only those pages with a particular Library item. Choose the Files That Use option from the Look In list. Next, pick the Library item to update.

4. To see the results from the update process, leave the Show Log check box selected.

5. When all your options are set, click the Start button. If you have the Show Log option selected—and I prefer to—you can follow the process.

6. Click the Close button when you're finished.

You should note that if you were working with a live site, you'd need to upload the pages on which changes were made. Dreamweaver includes a Synchronize command to automate this process.

CHAPTER 10

Using Templates and Reports

Ramp Up Your Productivity with Templates and Reports

Dreamweaver templates are very different from those found in FrontPage. FrontPage templates basically are just cookie-cutter molds. Unlike FrontPage, Dreamweaver templates are a mixture of locked and editable areas that are completely customizable. Like Library items, once you've made a change to a Dreamweaver template, that change is reflected in the pages derived from it.

The term *report* generally means a static output, either electronic or hard-copy. In Dreamweaver, however, a report not only lists the problem, it gives you direct access to it. Dreamweaver reports go far beyond FrontPage's spreadsheet-like reports in terms of what information is available. As you'll see later in this chapter, Dreamweaver's reporting capability is even extensible—as is evident in the extension emulating FrontPage reports.

What You'll Learn in This Chapter:
- How using templates and reports improves productivity
- How to create, edit, and update a template
- How to run FrontPage reports in Dreamweaver

Creating a Template from an Existing Page

The first step in creating a template from the current page couldn't be simpler. To begin, all you basically do is save the file. Because Dreamweaver templates are saved in a special folder called—you guessed it—Templates, the procedure is a little different from a regular file save. Let's try creating your first template:

▼ **Try It Yourself**

1. To practice, open *news.htm* from the Media folder for this chapter.

2. Choose File→Save As Template.

3. In the Save As Template dialog box, be sure you're saving to the right site; if not, you can choose any defined one from the Site list.

   You'll see a list of existing templates in the site, if any exist, as shown in Figure 10.1.

Figure 10.1
You can name templates anything you'd like when you save them.

4. Enter a unique name in the Save As field. Again, this is a name only for your reference, so make it as descriptive as you like. I'll use *News Master* for mine.

5. Click OK when you're finished.

Now you're ready to complete the template creation process by declaring which areas on your page should be editable.

Establishing Editable Regions

After you've saved a page as a template, you'll see double-angle brackets surrounding the word "Template" in the title bar, followed by the template name in parentheses. This makes it easy to distinguish templates from standard pages.

As I mentioned earlier, a template is made of locked and unlocked—or editable—regions. When you first create a template, everything is considered to be in a locked area, unless you specify otherwise. It's essential that you define at least one editable region. If you attempt to save your new template without doing so, Dreamweaver warns you that no editable regions were found. Templates without editable regions are pretty useless because you can only reproduce the same page over and over again.

Try It Yourself ▼

So, how does one mark an editable region? Glad you asked; here's how it's done:

1. In our template made from *news.htm*, begin by selecting the month and year after the word Headlines and the colon, as shown in Figure 10.2.

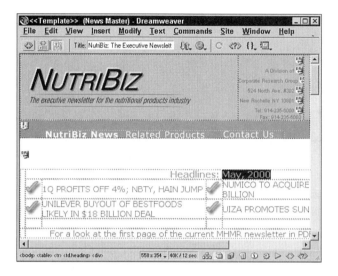

Figure 10.2
When you convert existing text to an editable region, you leave a placeholder that helps identify the expected content.

2. Choose Modify→Templates→New Editable Region.

3. In the dialog box, enter a unique name for the region. I'll use Month and Year.

4. After you click OK, you'll notice that the area is now marked with an outline and the name of the region is displayed onscreen (see Figure 10.2). You can toggle this off by choosing Visual Aids→Invisible Elements from the View Options button.

5. Next, I'll repeat the same procedure for each headline in the table. Be sure you select only the existing text.

6. Next, let's make the entire table following the headlines editable (including the phrase "The Battle for Shelf Space Has Begun") so we can add entirely new content. To do this, click anywhere in the table and then choose "table" from the Tag Selector.

7. Choose Modify→Templates→New Editable Region and pick a name for the area, like Center Content.

Note

One of the keys to working with templates is to leave as much repeated material as possible. I could have chosen the entire sentence, but because I know I'll always need the Headlines: portion, I'll leave that locked so I won't have to re-enter it every time.

Tip

Rather than use the main menus each time, I like to use the context menu. To do this, (Ctrl) [Right] click on the selected text and choose New Editable Region from the shortcut menu.

8. Finally, (Ctrl) [Right] click on the image of the woman with the laptop and make it an editable region. This will allow us to change the graphic but keep all the marketing text the same.

9. When you're finished, choose File→Save to store your new template.

There's one more technique to cover before we're ready to start using our templates: adding a new region without selecting anything. Although it's best to use placeholder text or graphics wherever possible, it's not always feasible—although, I find that placeholders make it easier for developers to remember what type of content goes where in a template. Dreamweaver enables you to place your cursor where you'd like to add an editable region and add one by choosing Modify→Templates→New Editable Region. The procedure is the same—you still need to enter a unique name for the region—and Dreamweaver still displays the name in a tab above the region. However, it also uses the name, enclosed in braces (curly brackets), as a placeholder. You must replace the placeholder text with your content; otherwise, users will just see the name in braces.

Creating a Document from a Template

Now that you have your template, complete with editable regions, you're ready to build a new page based on that template. You'll find that the editable regions are clearly marked, and you can navigate from one to another, similar to tabbing from one field to another in a form.

Managing your templates, like managing your Library items, is handled through Dreamweaver's Assets panel. Like the Library items, you'll see a preview of the template page and a list of available templates. Here's how you create a new document and begin changing the editable content:

1. Open the Assets panel and select the Template button, shown in Figure 10.3.

2. (Ctrl) [Right] click the template we've been working with, and choose New From Template from the context menu.

Figure 10.3
The Templates category of the Assets panel gives you a visual reference, as well as your descriptive name.

3. Move your cursor around the page. Notice that the cursor is active only over editable regions. Everywhere else, the cursor displays the universal "no access" symbol—a circle with a line through it—indicating the locked content.

4. Highlight the text in the first editable region, the month and the year. Replace the placeholder text with the current month and year.

5. Press Tab to move to the first placeholder headline. The placeholder text is automatically selected, and you can simply enter your new content.

6. Continue to replace all the headlines.

7. You'll find that you can't tab into the next editable region because it is a table rather than text. Instead of making any small changes, let's delete the entire item for this page. Click anywhere in the table, and then choose Table from the Tag Selector. Press Delete to remove the table.

8. Finally, let's change images. Double-click on the image of the woman with the laptop to open the Select Image Source dialog box. From the Media/images folder, choose *doctor2.jpg* and click Select.

9. Press F12 to preview your page. As you can see, there's no indication of the editable regions, just a great page.

10. Back in Dreamweaver, choose File→Save to store your work.

Note
You might notice that even though the image was a different width and height, Dreamweaver brought it into the layout without a hitch.

Although generating pages from templates is very cool, the next section explains an even better feature—updating templates.

Updating Templates

Try It Yourself ▼

Remember how you could change all the Library items embedded in your Web pages just by modifying the original Library item? You can do the same thing with templates—in fact, you even can use Library items in your templates.

1. To demonstrate, double-click the template we've been working with in the Template category of the Assets panel to open it for editing.

2. Scroll down to the bottom of the page.

3. Switch to the Library category of the Assets panel and drop in the copyright Library item created in the previous chapter.

4. Choose File—Save to store the template and automatically update any documents derived from the template, as shown in Figure 10.4.

Figure 10.4
Saving a changed template triggers the Update Templates dialog box.

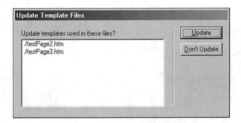

5. Now reopen the document we built based on this template and scroll down to the bottom.

Not only is the copyright text in place, but it also remains a Library item—so when it comes time to update it, the update will take place even in a template and template-derived document.

Using Template Themes from the Professional QuickStart Collection

As you can tell, Dreamweaver templates are extremely powerful and a wonderful way to streamline your Web site production.

Rather than rely on prebuilt templates, most professional designers construct their own—a very straightforward procedure in Dreamweaver. There are, however, a number of well-crafted templates available both from Macromedia and from third-party vendors.

Macromedia offers the Professional QuickStart Collection of emplates. Download the QuickStart Collection at *http://www.macromedia.com/software/dwfwstudio/download/collection/*. Ten professionally designed templates are included—all fully editable and ready to go. If you have Fireworks, you'll also be able to take advantage of the fully editable clip art collection.

After you've downloaded and uncompressed the QuickStart Collection, open the file *start.html* in your browser for an overview of what's available. If you'd like to use one of the 10 templates as a starting point, you have two options. You can either copy the particular Templates folder, and its contents, into an existing site, or you can define the template folder as a new site. Either way, the Templates folder and all the images are ready to go.

Running the FrontPage Reports in Dreamweaver

Dreamweaver Reports can give you crucial feedback about the structure and workings of your entire site. Better yet, Dreamweaver Reports are interactive, and you immediately can fix any problems flagged by the reports. Let's see how they work by checking which HTML files in our site are orphaned. We do this by running the Unlinked Files report.

▼ **Try It Yourself**

1. To open the Reports dialog box, choose Site→Reports.

2. Set the scope of the report by choosing Entire Local Site from the Report On list.

3. Under FrontPage Migration Kit, check the box next to Unlinked Files, as shown in Figure 10.5.

4. If a report has any user-configurable settings, the Report Settings button becomes active, as it has in this case. Click the Report Settings button now to see what's configurable.

Note

If you haven't installed the SiteSummaryReports extension, as detailed in Chapter 2, you'll need to do that before proceeding with the following section.

Figure 10.5
Select the reports you'd like to run; you can run as many as you like at one sitting.

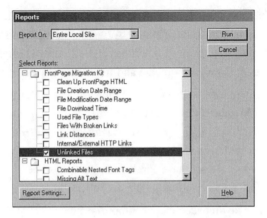

5. The settings dialog box for Unlinked Files allows us to specify which file types should be examined. Keep the default settings by clicking OK.

6. Click Run to execute your report.

   Dreamweaver replaces the Reports dialog box with the Results window as it examines all the HTML files in your site. Any file found that isn't connected to any other file in your site is listed as shown in Figure 10.6.

Figure 10.6
You can open any files listed in the Results window by double-clicking it.

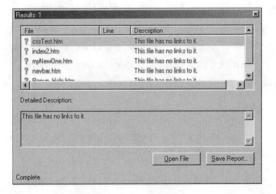

7. To open a listed file, just double-click its entry. Some reports, like Untitled Documents, not only open the page, they go right to the line of code with the problem!

8. You can save the report in an XML format by clicking the Save Report button.

In all, there are eight reports under the FrontPage Migration Kit group. All but one—Used File Types—have some sort of Report Settings available. Most are self-explanatory, but if you need assistance, click the Help button from the Report Settings dialog box.

CHAPTER 11

Publishing Web Pages with Dreamweaver

Getting Your Site Live with Dreamweaver

No Web site is complete until it's been published and is available for viewing by its intended audience, whether that's the general public or a select intranet group. Dreamweaver calls transferring files from the local to the remote site *putting* files, whereas moving files the other direction—from the remote to the local site—is known as *getting* files.

Dreamweaver gives you far more direct control over what's published—or put—than FrontPage. Professional Web designers typically make publishing files to the server part of an ongoing testing process, rather than waiting until the entire site is completed before uploading all the files at one time. Frequently, the files are transferred to a staging server where they can be viewed and checked before the site goes live and is available to the public. Dreamweaver makes it easy for you to publish just the HTML files while it handles the images, scripts, linked stylesheets, and so on.

What You'll Learn in This Chapter:
- How to publish your Dreameaver site
- How to change links sitewide

Publishing Individual Pages

With the Dreamweaver Site window's two-pane setup—one side for the remote files and the other for the local ones—it's easy to understand the publishing process. Select files in the local side and put them on the remote side. There are numerous ways to put the files:

- You can drag and drop them.
- You can click a Put button.
- You can use a menu option (Site→Put).

- You can use a keyboard shortcut: (Command-Shift-U) [Ctrl+Shift+U]; think "u" for "upload."

Try It Yourself ▼

Let's step through a typical publishing session so you can see how it works:

1. Switch to the Site window by selecting the Site icon in the Launcher or by choosing Window→Site Files.

2. Select one or more HTML files from the file list.

3. Click the Put button in the toolbar on top of the Site window. (Of course, you could use any of the other methods mentioned.) Dreamweaver will connect to the server.

4. A dialog box appears asking if you want to transfer the dependent files too, as shown in Figure 11.1. Click Yes.

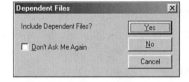

Figure 11.1
Let Dreamweaver transfer all the dependent files to avoid missing any.

Note

As you know, an HTML file can be composed of many other files, mostly those of graphics, but often other media files or code files also are involved. When you opt to transfer the dependent files—and you always should when the site is first published—▲ Dreamweaver not only automatically transfers all the other files needed to create the HTML page, it also replicates the local site folder structure, as needed, on the remote site. This process ensures that the two sites will mirror each other.

5. If there are many files, you can follow the progress on the indicator in the lower right of the screen. If you encounter a problem and need to stop the transfer, click the Stop button.

6. The bottom status bar tells you what's happening and which files are being transferred. When the process is complete, you can use your browser to test the files.

7. When you're finished putting files on the remote site, click the Connect button to break the connection.

While designers spend most of their file transfer time putting files from the local site to the remote, sometimes the traffic must flow in the other direction. In the next section, you'll see how the parallel process—getting files—works.

Getting Files from the Server

One question beginning Web designers often get stuck on is "How do I work on an existing site?" If you don't have access to the original files—not an uncommon situation, I'm afraid—one way to get started is to use Dreamweaver to get all the files from the remote server to your local design station.

Getting files is almost identical to putting them—instead of moving files from the right pane to the left, you're moving them from the left to the right. Similar methods for getting files are available:

- You can drag and drop them.
- You can click a Get button.
- You can use a menu option (Site→Get).
- You can use a keyboard shortcut—(Command-Shift-D) [Ctrl+Shift+D]; think "d" for "download."

When you're getting files, you'll also encounter the Include Dependent Files dialog box. Again, you can choose to do this on a case-by-case basis. If you already have all the dependent files, there's no need to download them again and you'll save yourself a fair amount of time by choosing No on the alert.

Here's an example of getting a file:

▼ **Try It Yourself**

1. If you don't have files showing in the remote file view, click the Connect button.

   When you have files displayed on both sides of the Site window, you're ready to get the remote files.

2. Select a file or two on the remote side and drag them over to the local side.

3. Once again, Dreamweaver asks whether you'd like to Include Dependent Files in the transfer—this time, we'll assume we already have the graphics and we'll say No.

4. After the files are transferred, click the Connect button again to disconnect from the remote site.

Changing Links Sitewide

If you rename a file or move it to another folder location, Dreamweaver automatically updates all the associated links. For example, if you want to "clean up" your site before it's published, and move all your images and graphic files from the root directory into another folder called images, use the Site window to drag the files to their new folder. Dreamweaver will ask if you want to update all the links—click Yes.

Aside from this automatic method, you also can manually modify a link throughout the site by using the Change Link Sitewide command. When altering page links, this command can only be used with site root relative links, such as */myPage.htm*, or absolute links, such as *http://www.BigCo.com/myPage.htm*. (If you need to alter a relative link, Dreamweaver has a fantastic Find and Replace command that will do the trick.)

Let's say on every page in your site, there is a Special Sale button that links to the department having the biggest sale that month. Because you can't link to a single page, you'll need to change the sale link on every page. Here's how you would do it:

Try It Yourself

1. Switch to the Site window.

2. In the site file list, locate the file currently being linked to that you want to change and select it.

3. Choose Site→Change Link Sitewide.

4. In the dialog box that opens (see Figure 11.2), you'll see that the first field already has been filled in. Now, locate the file you want to make the new target of all your links by clicking the folder icon next to the second field.

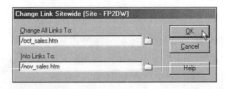

Figure 11.2
The Change Link Sitewide command works with site root relative, absolute, or mailto: links.

5. Click OK and Dreamweaver displays a list of files to update. To modify them all—and you should—click Update. If you

want to update just some of them, select those files from the list, and then click Update.

6. When Dreamweaver is finished changing the links, you'll need to upload the updated files. Probably the easiest way to do this is to choose Edit→Select Newer Local, and then choose the Put button. You won't need to upload the dependent files at this time.

Tip
Something that makes this feature especially useful is that you also can use the Change Link Sitewide to update mailto: links.

▲

CHAPTER 12

Extending Dreamweaver

Dreamweaver and Automation

I'll admit it—I'm a real freak when it comes to macros and other automation tools. Anything I can do to speed up my work, I'll try. And Dreamweaver has plenty of extensible power to feed my automation addiction. Aside from the architectural openness that enables all sorts of extensions, Dreamweaver also makes it easy for the common users to automate their workflow.

In this chapter, you'll learn how to work with the History panel to repeat your actions—much like macros in FrontPage. You'll also be introduced to the wide world of extensions available on the Dreamweaver Exchange.

What You'll Learn in This Chapter:
- How to automate tasks
- What the History panel is used for

Using the History Panel to Replay Steps

A Web designer often has to repeat the same basic set of operations again and again. Dreamweaver's History panel can take any set of actions and replay them in sequence, so that you quickly can automate your work.

The History panel's replay feature is not without limitation, however. Dreamweaver cannot replay any steps that involve a mouse selection on the Document window. You can, however, record and play back any keystrokes—and there are a fair number of mouse equivalents available.

Let's look at an example:

▼ **Try It Yourself**

1. Choose Window→History, or select the History panel icon (the right-facing triangle) from the Launcher. The History panel opens, as shown in Figure 12.1.

Figure 12.1
Dreamweaver's History panel allows you to automate many production tasks.

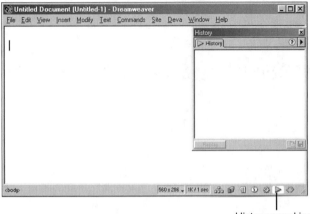

History panel icon

2. Open page *history_ex.htm* from this chapter's Media folder.

   In the table on the page, the last column of figures should be aligned to the decimal point, in order to look right. Unfortunately, there is no such thing as a decimal tab in HTML. To begin to compensate for that lack, you could right-align the cells.

3. Place your cursor in the first cell with the dollar figure in it and choose the Right alignment button from the Property inspector.

   Notice how the History panel immediately shows the command Text Alignment: Right, as shown in Figure 12.2. Although the right alignment command applied to all the cells would align them all, it's really too far over. Let's use nonbreaking spaces to push it back over to the left a bit.

Figure 12.2
The History panel tracks every command issued.

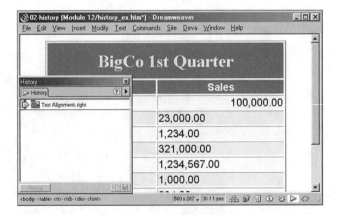

4. Press the End key to move to the end of the cell.

5. Press (Command-Shift-Spacebar) [Ctrl+Shift+Spacebar] 10 times to move the dollar amount more to the center of the cell, but keep it aligned.

   We've entered the two basic actions we want to repeat—right align and inserting non-breaking spaces. However, one of the keys to using the History panel for automation is to set up the next iteration of the command so that you can automate your work as much as possible.

6. Press the down arrow to go to the cell directly beneath the current one.

7. Press the End key to move to the last character in the cell. We're ready to replay our previous commands—and, if it works, keep on going.

8. In the History panel, select the first command in the series: Text Alignment: Right. You might have to scroll up to see it.

9. Press Shift and scroll down to the bottom of the History panel to select the last command: End of Line.

10. Click the History panel's Replay button once. The dollar amount in the current cell aligns with the one above, and the cursor now moves into position for the next figure. The command Replay Steps is shown in the History panel, as can be seen in Figure 12.3.

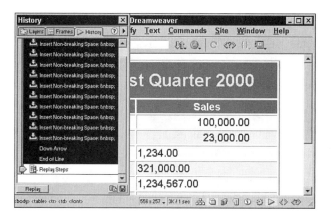

Figure 12.3
Use the Replay button to repeat selected steps.

Continue clicking the Replay button until all the figures are aligned. Be careful not to run the command when the cursor is in the top row. However, if you do, you can always drag the pointer upward in the History panel, undoing the last action.

Saving History Steps As Commands

Note
If you've already saved and closed the previous lesson, you'll have to repeat the initial steps for aligning our figures. If not, the steps will still be available in the History panel.

Replaying selected actions in the History panel is great for single-document automation, but how do you apply the same actions to another document? Luckily, Dreamweaver enables you to save any set of selected steps as a command. The new command is then instantly listed and available from the Commands menu, regardless of the current page or site. These instant commands can be renamed or removed at any time.

Try It Yourself ▼

Let's convert our steps from the previous lesson into a command and apply it to another page:

1. Continue working with the material from the previous lesson.

2. With the necessary steps chosen, click the Save As Command button found on the bottom right of the History panel, shown in Figure 12.4.

Figure 12.4
When converted to a command, the selected History steps will always be available.

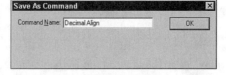

3. In the Save As Command dialog box, name your command as you want it to appear in the menu.

Note
Here's one place you don't have to be worried about using spaces; for example, I named this command "Decimal Align."

4. To test the command, open *history_ex2.htm* from this chapter's Media folder.

5. Place your cursor at the end of the cell with the first dollar figure in it.

6. Choose Commands→Decimal Align (or whatever you called your command).

7. Repeat step 6 for every dollar figure in the column.

If you ever need to rename or delete your custom command, choose Commands→Edit Command List.

Automating your workflow is something to always keep in the back of your mind as a possibility. Not only does it save time, but it also adds consistency to your documents.

Accessing the Macromedia Dreamweaver Exchange

As a parting gift, I want to introduce you to a tremendous resource for Dreamweaver users, the Dreamweaver Exchange, hosted by Macromedia. The Exchange is a part of Macromedia's main Web site, which maintains a searchable collection of Dreamweaver extensions. You easily can access the Exchange by choosing Help→Dreamweaver Exchange or Commands→Get More Commands.

The first time you visit the Exchange, it's a good idea to go ahead and register so you can take advantage of what the Exchange has to offer. And what the Exchange has to offer is hundreds and hundreds of extensions—all kinds of extensions: commands, behaviors, objects, Flash button styles, templates, and plenty more. The extensions are categorized so you easily can find what you need.

All the extensions on the Exchange have been checked by Macromedia to be sure they do what they claim and that they're safe; that is, that they are virus-free. Certain extensions have a Macromedia approval seal, which means they conform to the Dreamweaver user interface guidelines. On the Exchange, you also can find download stats, ratings, and discussion threads for each extension to help you decide whether the extension is right for you. The vast majority of the extensions are free, and all are installed via the Extension Manager, which we used to install the FrontPage extensions in Chapter 2, "Defining a Site."

Bottom line: If you find yourself working in Dreamweaver and thinking, "There must be a way to do this…" chances are there is—and chances are you'll find your answer on the Exchange.

In Conclusion

Although all the material we covered might seem like a lot to master, I'm sure you can do it. I've found it's best to work with one concept at a time and, if you can, apply it to a project you're involved with. Not only does this get the work done, but most folks seem to retain information they've gained in accomplishing a meaningful task.

If you get stuck, be sure to visit Macromedia's support site, which you can access by choosing Help→Dreamweaver Support. You also should feel free to e-mail me with your questions and—although I don't promise instant turnaround—I'll try to help you however I can. You can reach me at *jlowery@idest.com*.

Good luck with Dreamweaver—it's an exciting, ever-evolving program with a lot to offer. Keep on Dreaming and Weaving...

Glossary

A

action JavaScript code inserted into a Web page. Actions are what happens when events are triggered.

align The term used to specify where your page elements appear. Images can be aligned to the left, right, or center of a page, layer, or table; they also can be aligned vertically in relation to the text in a paragraph.

anchor A specified point on a page to which you can link so that the page opens to that particular spot rather than to the top of the page.

asset Any element that is part of a Web site. Assets are all the images, templates, library items, movies, colors, and URLs that make up the site. Dreamweaver collects all the information about your site and displays a categorized list of assets in the **Assets** panel.

authoring tool The aspect of Dreamweaver that allows you to add scripts and animations wherever and whenever you want them.

B

background color A color that displays while the background image is loading. Specify a background color for your pages so that your text will be visible even if the background image fails to load. If you want a solid-color background, do not specify an image.

background image An image that tiles (repeats in a tilelike fashion) to fill the background of a page.

BASEFONT The default size of the text you type in a document window. You can change the size of the font on the page by specifying a particular font size or by sizing the text relative to the BASEFONT size.

GLOSSARY

baseline The imaginary line on which the base of letters rests. Descenders in letters such as *g* or *q* dip below the baseline.

baseline shift The moving of selected letters to positions above or below the baseline (the line on which the letters rest) to create subscript and superscript characters within your text.

behavior A JavaScript script that allows you to create interactive Web pages easily in Dreamweaver.

Behaviors Inspector A Dreamweaver window that allows you to attach, check, and modify any behaviors you have set.

bevel A special effect that you can apply to an object in Fireworks.

BMP A Windows bitmap image format that features low quality and large file sizes. BMP images are used for screen backgrounds. Not suitable for display on Web pages.

button A form element. Buttons are used to perform actions such as activating a search, resetting the form, or submitting the completed form to the server. You can change the text on the button face to make it clear what the action of the button is. The action of the button is controlled by the form handling script.

C

cache A storage space in memory or on the hard disk that Dreamweaver uses to help manage the site and to ensure that links are kept up to date. When you first create a site, you can specify that a cache be created along with the site. In Dreamweaver, the **Assets** panel requires a disk cache so that it can assemble and sort pertinent data for the site.

cell padding In a table, the amount of space between an object contained in a cell and the border of the cell.

cell spacing The amount of space between two cells in a table.

check box A form element. Forms typically use multiple check boxes when more than one answer is acceptable, as in a list of preferences. A single check box can be used for yes and no answers or to enable or disable an option. The user clicks the check box to place a tick mark in the box.

color depth The maximum number of colors available for the image. A GIF file, for example, can have a maximum of 256 colors; a JPEG file can have millions of colors; and a PNG file can also have millions of colors.

command A series of actions saved as a single named action that you can apply over and over again—to elements in a single document or to elements in multiple documents.

crop To cut away unwanted areas of an image to focus the viewer's attention on the desired subject.

CSS (Cascading Style Sheets) styles CSS styles are custom created for a site and are used to control the way that page elements are displayed. From formatting text to adding borders and backgrounds to tables and text, CSS can be used to guarantee consistency in your site.

D

definition list A list in which the word being defined appears left-justified, with the definition on the following line, slightly indented.

delimiter A character that separates information in table fields or a spreadsheet. Commas and tabs are the two most common delimiters used.

DHTML (Dynamic Hypertext Markup Language) A programming language that gives you the flexibility to lay out and create interactive Web pages.

distort To change an image's dimension with no regard for ratio or appearance. Distorting an image is an easy way to add interest to a simple graphic or to text.

dither The process by which an application tries to reproduce a color that it can't otherwise display by using alternating pixels of two other colors. You can set how carefully the application tries to produce the missing color by setting a dither percentage. The greater the percentage, the closer the result is to the missing color.

docking The process of combining panels into a single floating panel. Each panel is represented by tabs at the top of the floating panel; click a tab to display that panel.

E

editable region On a template, this is a region that has been designated specifically as an area that can be changed. If the area on the template has not been designated as an editable region, that area cannot be changed.

element An item on a page, such as a graphic or text.

emboss A special effect that you can apply to an object in Fireworks.

event In a script, the incident that triggers the action. For example, you might want a particular action to occur when the user clicks a button; the button click is the event that triggers the scripted action.

Exchange The online site provided by Macromedia where you can go to get easy-to-install extensions that add new features to Dreamweaver. You can access the Exchange from the main screen of the Dreamweaver Support Center site.

export To take a file from its native application and prepare it for use in another application. For example, you can create a graphics file in Fireworks, save it in the Fireworks native PNG format, and then export the file to Dreamweaver as a GIF file.

extension Sometimes called an "add-in" or a "plug-in." Extensions provide additional features for your Dreamweaver software. Many extensions can be downloaded from the Macromedia Exchange at *http://www.macromedia.com/exchange/dreamweaver/*. These downloadable extensions are categorized by type and cover everything from DHTML effects to the latest browser profiles. Make sure that you download extensions for Dreamweaver version 4. The site will tell you which version of Dreamweaver the extensions work with.

external hyperlink A hyperlink that links to a page within a different site.

F

file extension The last part of a filename that identifies the type of file. Web pages have an `.htm` or `.html` extension, Word files have a `.doc` extension, and so on. In Dreamweaver, the term *extension* also refers to the add-ons you can download to give the user additional functionality.

file field   A form element. A file field is a specific kind of text box that accepts the pathname to a file or folder. A file field comes with a Browse button that the user can click to locate files or folders on the local machine. Forms use file fields so that users can specify the location to which they want to download files or from which they want to upload files. Before you use a file field on a form, check with your hosting company to make sure that your server can accept a file attached to a form.

font family   A generic name for a group of similar fonts. Most computers acknowledge these font families: cursive, fantasy, monospace, sans serif, and serif. If a browser cannot display any of the specific fonts you have chosen, the browser will display the text using the default font associated with the font family.

form   A container object that holds all your form elements (text boxes, radio buttons, and so on). Forms are used to collect data and information from site visitors.

form elements   The parts of a form—the text fields, check boxes, and radio buttons—that the visitor fills in or selects.

form field validation   A behavior that checks whether the visitor to a form has entered the right kind of information in the form fields and ensures that necessary information has not been omitted. The validation behavior is executed when the visitor clicks the Submit button on the form.

frames   Individual Web pages held together in sets. When the browser sees them, it draws the frames together to give the impression of a single page.

frameset   An HTML page that holds all the information for all the frames you want to appear together. When you create a frameset, you must also create the individual pages to be displayed as frames.

G

GIF (graphics image format) An image format that is ideal for small files using minimal colors. The GIF format can support up to 256 colors as well as the use of transparency. GIF files are ideal for buttons, lines, and backgrounds.

GIF animation file A single GIF file created from multiple frames. GIF animations are ideal for Web pages because they have small file sizes.

glow A special effect you can apply to an object in Fireworks.

gridlines Lines that display on your page as squares set to a size of your choice. Gridlines can be used with or without the rulers to help you achieve exact placement of elements and layers on the page.

H

head content The title information about the page. The head section also contains any metatags that you add to your site and is commonly used for holding references to scripts.

hidden field A form element. Hidden fields usually contain information used by the server when it processes the form. The user cannot see or change the information contained in the hidden field.

home page The first page that visitors to your site see. The home page in your site has the filename *index.html* or *default.html*.

hosting company The company that hosts your Web site. This can be your ISP or a specific hosting company that offers the services you require. If you want to use CGI or ASP scripts, make sure that the hosting service you intend to use offers support for these technologies before signing up with it.

hotspot In a larger graphic image that functions as an imagemap or a navigational tool for the site, one of the areas that actually links to another page or site. For example, if you have an imagemap of a U.S. map, each state can be a hotspot that, when clicked, links to a page or site about that particular state.

HTML editor The aspect of Dreamweaver in which you input your page content and can change the HTML code that actually creates the Web page.

HTML styles A named group of formatting elements that you can apply to text and paragraphs in a site. Styles are a way to ensure consistent formatting of the text in your site. After you create an HTML style, you can reuse it.

hyperlink An image or a clickable piece of text that takes the site visitor to another page or reference in the site, to another Web site, or to an open email application.

I

image field A form element. An image field can consist of any appropriately sized graphic image. When the user clicks the graphic, the action assigned to the graphic occurs, just as it does when you click a normal button.

imagemap A single image with areas that are actually links to other pages or sites. For example, you can have a graphic of a pirate ship on your site's home page. Clicking the skull and crossbones can link the visitor to a list of banner vendors; clicking the carved figurehead on the front of the pirate ship can link to a list of woodworkers; clicking the trapdoor can link to an online version of a popular dungeons-and-dragons game.

instance A copy of a symbol (located in the library) that can be used over and over again.

internal hyperlink A hyperlink that links to a page within the same site.

J

JPEG (Joint Photographic Experts Group) The best format for photographs because JPEG files contain millions of colors. JPEG images don't give you the option of including transparency or interlaced images, but they do allow you to specify the degree of file compression so that you can create a balance between image quality and file size.

jump menu A form element. A jump menu is a list of hyperlinks presented on the form as a drop-down menu. When the user makes a choice from the drop-down menu, a hyperlink is activated. Items on the jump menu can link to other pages within the site or to external pages elsewhere on the Internet.

K

kerning   Changing the amount of space between two or more letters to make the letters look less tight or less airy. This adjustment feature is especially handy with large fonts and for letter combinations that don't fit together well (such as *AW*).

keyboard shortcut   A keyboard equivalent for using the mouse to open a menu and select a command. For example, pressing **Ctrl+F2** (⌘**+F2** on the Mac) is the keyboard shortcut for opening the **Window** menu and selecting **Objects** (both approaches open the **Objects** panel).

keyframe   One of the white circles along the animation marker in the timelines panel. The keyframe markers indicate where the animation starts, stops, or changes direction during the course of the animation.

L

Launcher   One of the panels most commonly used in Dreamweaver. This panel contains buttons for opening and closing other panels and windows.

layer   A container or holder for page content. Layers can hold any page element, have their own properties and settings, and also have the advantage of being positioned exactly on the page. In Web design terms, layers are still an innovation, implemented quite recently into the vocabulary of Web designers and developers. The idea behind layers was to give designers complete control over the appearance of the content of the pages at all times.

leading   The amount of space between lines of text (in other words, the line spacing).

Library   A folder for a site that contains all the page elements you use or update frequently. Also the location in the **Assets** panel that permits the storage of elements you want to reuse in your site. If you insert items on your pages from the library, you can update all those pages simply by updating the element in the Library. The Library then traces the item's links to pages in the site and updates the pages with the new version of the item.

library items The page elements (images, text, and so on) contained in the Library folder for a site.

link *See* hyperlink.

list A form element. A list offers a scrollable list of options from which the user can select multiple options. *See also* menu.

local folder How Dreamweaver refers to the location on your hard disk that contains all the files used to create the current Web site.

lossless A compression technique that makes large graphics or audio files smaller without noticeable loss of data. The ubiquitous WinZip program, for example, compresses files without losing any of the data in the files.

lossy A compression technique that makes large graphics or audio files smaller by actually dropping some information from the file. (For example,

you can save a large color graphic file to a smaller size by removing some of the colors.) The JPEG compression technique uses the lossy method to make smaller file sizes.

M–N

menu A form element. A menu offers a drop-down list of options from which the user can select only one. *See also* list.

metatags The term used for keywords and descriptions used by search engines to locate sites that match a search request.

multiframe editing A feature in Fireworks that enables you to edit the visible contents of any frame. If you have turned on the onion skinning feature, you can edit the content of any frame you see in the document window—not just the content of the currently selected frame.

navigation bar A collection of buttons that have been saved as a group to create a navigation system for a Web site.

navigation frame A separate frame on a page in which lists of links to other pages in the Web site can be found. Because the navigation frame remains onscreen even when other pages are displayed in the main frame, the links in the navigation frame can be accessed at any time, making the navigation frame an easy way for visitors to navigate through your site.

nested frameset   A frameset within another frameset.

nested tables   A table inserted inside another table. For example, you might use one table as a design element for your page; you might want to insert into that table another table of information. The second table is "nested" within the design table.

O

Objects panel   One of the panels most commonly used in Dreamweaver. The Objects panel has six categories, each of which offers shortcuts to menu commands and other actions.

onion skinning   A common technique when working with animations. In simple terms, it allows you to see the contents of more than one frame at a time. Onion skinning can help you move an object a certain distance from one frame to the next; the "ghost images" of the objects in the frames before and after the current frame help you position the objects in the current frame.

option button   *See* radio button.

P–Q

padding   *See* cell padding.

page properties   The default properties for the pages in a site. You can specify these properties in the **Page Properties** dialog box. Properties include the title of the page, the background color and image for the page, text and link colors, and margins.

panel   A collection of tools used for performing functions or actions. For example, the Objects panel allows you to insert various objects into your pages.

PCX   Originally developed by Zsoft for its PCpaintbrush program, PCX is a graphics file format for graphics programs running on PCs. This format is not suitable for display on Web pages.

PNG An image format similar to the GIF format that is the default file format for graphics files created in Fireworks. PNG files can have millions of colors and are more effective at compressing files with large areas of solid color than JPEG files are.

progressive JPEG A version of a JPEG file that acts like an interlaced GIF file. When a progressive JPEG file loads on a Web page, a low-resolution version of the file appears first and continues to improve as the file completes the download process.

properties The information about the currently selected page element. Image properties include the source reference, dimensions, and any Alt text. Text properties include the color, font, and size of the text.

Properties Inspector One of the panels most commonly used in Dreamweaver. When you select an element on the page, you can view the properties for that element in the Properties Inspector.

R

radio button A form element. Radio buttons are used when the visitor must choose only one of several options (as when choosing an age category on a personal information form). When you build a form that includes radio buttons, you must group the associated radio buttons together.

resample To change the resolution. Resampling an image object adds or removes pixels as required to make the image larger or smaller. Resampling a path object causes it to be redrawn at a larger size with minimum loss of quality.

rollover The effect caused by moving a mouse pointer over a Web-page button. The original button might be red, but hovering the mouse pointer over the button might change the button to green; clicking the button might cause the button to turn purple and then black as it remains in the "pressed in" position. These color changes are one example of a button rollover effect.

ruler A convenient measurement tool that you can display in the document window to show exactly where each and every element has been placed. Rulers are particularly handy if you are not accustomed to using the pixel measurement system. Although rulers can be displayed in centimeters and inches, they appear in pixels by default.

S

script A dedicated piece of JavaScript or other language coding that performs a task in your Web page. Scripts are usually JavaScript or CGI (common gateway interface) and are used for everything from handling and processing forms to checking which browser a site visitor is using.

site manager The aspect of Dreamweaver that lets you see all your Web site files at a glance.

skew To slant an image either vertically or horizontally (or both). Skewing an image is an easy way to add interest to a simple graphic or text.

slice An individual part of an image file. Slices can be optimized individually, can have hotspots attached, and are used in the creation of rollovers. Slices can be edited individually, meaning that you can use the same images from file to file and change only the required slices.

spacing *See* cell spacing.

style A group of formatting options that can be applied to elements on the page to make the formatting of those elements consistent. For example, you can create a style that formats a paragraph of text in a certain way (with a certain font, size, and color). If you apply that style to all paragraphs of text on the page, the document will be formatted consistently.

symbol An object that is stored in the Library.

T–V

tabular data Information created in another application (such as Microsoft Excel) and saved in a delimited format (comma or tab separated).

target A link that specifies which frame or window a

page displays in when it opens.

template   Predesigned Web pages on which you can model additional Web pages. Dreamweaver does not come with templates; you can, however, make your own templates that you can use to build all the pages for your site. Templates make it easy to design a complete site with consistent elements.

text box   A form element. A text box is a bound field into which visitors to the form can type free-form responses. Text boxes can be formatted to a specific size to allow a maximum number of characters and to allow the visitor to enter a single line or multiple lines of text. Text boxes can be designated as password boxes, meaning that characters the visitor types are disguised as asterisks as they appear on the screen.

text slice   A slice of an image that contains only text. You can edit the text in the text slice in Dreamweaver, even if the image was created or modified in Fireworks.

thumbnail   A smaller version of a graphic that, when clicked, opens to a larger version of the same image. Thumbnail versions of images download quickly and allow your site visitors to decide which images they want to see enlarged. If you use thumbnail images, you actually must have two versions of the same image available: one larger and one smaller.

TIFF (Tagged Image File Format)   The only file format that can be edited on both PC and Macintosh machines. Not suitable for display on Web pages.

tracing image   A Dreamweaver feature that allows you to copy a page layout from a graphic "mock-up." Use the tracing image as a screen background and position elements and images exactly on top of it. The tracing image is only displayed in Dreamweaver.

trigger   An event that tells Dreamweaver when to begin a particular action or animation. For example, the trigger that tells an animation on a page to start can be the loading of the page.

tweening   In creating animations, a process by which Fireworks creates the movement between frames for you.

W–Z

window A pane or special box that shows you information about a certain aspect of your page or site. For example, the **Site** window shows all the files in your current site, and the **HTML Source** window shows the code behind your current page.

Z index A value that indicates the order in which a particular layer appears in the "stack" of layers on the page. The higher the Z index value a layer has, the higher up in the stack of layers that layer will appear.

APPENDIX A

Keyboard Shortcuts

Managing Files

Action	Windows	Macintosh
New document	Control+N	Command-N
Open an HTML file	Control+O, or drag the file from the Explorer or Site window to the Document window	Command-O
Open in frame	Control+Shift+O	Command-Shift-O
Close	Control+W	Command-W
Save	Control+S	Command-S
Save as	Control+Shift+S	Command-Shift-S
Check links	Shift+F8	Command-F8
Exit/Quit	Control+Q	Command-Q

Inserting Objects

To Insert	Windows	Macintosh
Any object (image, Shockwave movie, and so on)	Drag file from the Explorer or Site window to the Document window	Drag file from the Finder or Site window to the Document window
Image	Control+Alt+I	Command-Option-I
Table	Control+Alt+T	Command-Option-T
Flash movie	Control+Alt+F	Command-Option-F
Shockwave Director movie	Control+Alt+D	Command-Option-D
Named anchor	Control+Alt+A	Command-Option-A

Viewing Panels

To Toggle the Display Of	Windows	Macintosh
Objects	Control+F2	Command-F2
Properties	Control+F3	Command-F3
Show/Hide Floating panels	F4	F4
Minimize all windows	Shift+F4	N/A
Restore all windows	Alt+Shift+F4	N/A

Previewing in Browser

Action	Windows	Macintosh
Preview in primary browser	F12	F12
Preview in secondary browser	Control+F12	Command-F12

General Editing

Action	Windows	Macintosh
Undo	Control+Z	Command-Z
Redo	Control+Y or Control+Shift+Z	Command-Y or Command-Shift-Z
Cut	Control+X or Shift+Del	Command-X or Shift-Del
Copy	Control+C or Control+Ins	Command-C or Command-Ins
Paste	Control+V or Shift+Ins	Command-V or Shift-Ins
Clear	Delete	Delete
Select All	Control+A	Command-A
Find and Replace	Control+F	Command-F
Find Next	F3	Command-G
Preferences	Control+U	Command-U

Text Editing

Action	Windows	Macintosh
Create a new paragraph	Enter	Return
Insert a line break 	Shift+Enter	Shift-Return
Insert a nonbreaking space	Control+Shift+Spacebar	Option-Spacebar

Action	Windows	Macintosh
Move text or object to another place in the page	Drag selected item to new location	Drag selected item to new location
Copy text or object to another place in the page	Control-drag selected item to new location	Option-drag selected item to new location
Select a word	Double-click	Double-click
Add selected items to library	Control+Shift+B	Command-Shift-B
Switch between design view and code editors	Control+Tab	Option-Tab
Open and close the Property inspector	Control+Shift+J	Command-Shift-J
Check spelling	Shift+F7	Shift-F7

Formatting Text

Action	Windows	Macintosh
Indent	Control+]	Command-]
Outdent	Control+[	Command-[
Format > None	Control+0 (zero)	Command-0 (zero)
Paragraph Format	Control+Shift+P	Command-Shift-P
Apply Headings 1 through 6 to a paragraph	Control+1 through 6	Command-1 through 6
Alignment > Left	Control+Shift+Alt+L	Command-Shift-Option-L
Alignment > Center	Control+Shift+Alt+C	Command-Shift-Option-C
Alignment > Right	Control+Shift+Alt+R	Command-Shift-Option-R
Make selected text bold	Control+B	Command-B
Make selected text italic	Control+I	Command-I
Edit Style Sheet	Control+Shift+E	Command-Shift-E

Image Editing

Action	Windows	Macintosh
Change image source attribute	Double-click image	Double-click image
Edit image in external editor	Control+double-click image	Command-double-click image

Link Editing

Action	Windows	Macintosh
Create hyperlink (select text)	Control+L	Command-L
Remove hyperlink	Control+Shift+L	Command-Shift-L
Drag and drop to create a hyperlink from a document	Select the text, image, or object, then Shift-drag the selection to a file in the Site window	Select the text, image, or object, then Shift-drag the selection to a file in the Site window
Drag and drop to create a hyperlink using the Property inspector	Select the text, image, or object, then drag the point-to-file icon in Property inspector to a file in the Site window	Select the text, image, or object, then drag the point-to-file icon in Property inspector to a file in the Site window
Open the linked-to document in Dreamweaver	Control+double-click link	Command-double-click link
Check links selected	Shift+F8	Shift-F8
Check links in the entire site	Control+F8	Command-F8

Getting Help

Action	Windows	Macintosh
Using Dreamweaver Help Topics	F1	F1
Reference	Shift+F1	Shift-F1
Dreamweaver Support Center	Control+F1	Command-F1

APPENDIX B

What's on the CD-ROM

This book's CD-ROM contains more than 60 minutes of full-screen video training with the interactivity of the Web! Learning to design a professional site has never been easier!

If you like what you learn, you may unlock the additional lessons for a *significant discount*, offered only to purchasers of this book. Use the CD-ROM and special code listed as follows to go to the Web site that offers you more than 60 minutes of free lessons, plus an exclusive discount off the upgraded training.

Code: Que001

Some of the content found in the book and in the CD training includes instructions on how to

- Convert your site from FrontPage
- Format and add text to your Web pages
- Create absolute, relative, and e-mail links
- Add and optimize images for your site
- Add templates and reports to make site building easier
- Publish your pages to the Web and manage your site from a server
- Use the Dreamweaver extensions from the Macromedia Exchange

To begin using the training or to obtain the author's project files, place the CD-ROM into a computer that is connected to the Internet—**but don't launch your Web browser**—instead, double-click on the Launch button on the CD-ROM and the training will begin within minutes.

With the easy-to-use interface, you can automatically navigate to different lessons from the left sidebar, or access the supplementary resources from the Resources tab.

Additionally, to work right alongside the author you can easily download the files by clicking on the Project Files tab.

INDEX

Symbols

  tag, 34
(basefont) tag, 38-39
(br) tag, 36

A

absolute font sizes, 37
absolute links, 73
actions, 93, 121
    automated, saving, 124-125
    Check links, 141
    Close, 141
    Exit/Quit, 141
    initiating, with browsers, 96
    New document, 141
    Open an HTML file, 141
    Open in frame, 141
    Save, 141
    Save as, 141
Add Browser dialog box, 89
adding
    behaviors (Dreamweaver), 93
    text, paragraphs, 33-34
aligning
    images, 58
    text, 41
        shortcut, 144
Apply Source Formatting option, 28
Apply to Extensions field, 28
assets, viewing, 56
Assets panel, 56, 99
    managing templates, 108
    Web site components, categorizing, 56
attaching, behaviors (Dreamweaver), 94-95
attributes
    border controls, 59-60
    displaying, 57
    horizontal space, 59
    margin controls, 59-60
    modifying, using Property inspector, 57
    vertical space, 59
automating, tasks, 121-124
Autostretch feature, 85

B

background graphics, 53, 63-65
    inserting, 63-64
behaviors (Dreamweaver), 93
    actions, 93
    adding, 93
    attaching, 94-95
    custom dialog box, 94
    deleting, 96-97
    events, 93
        modifying, 95-96
    modifying, 96-97
    testing, 95
Behaviors panel, 93, 98
block element, defined, 34
body copy, 33
bold, text, shortcut, 144
bookmarks (FrontPage). *See* named anchors
broken links, 73
Browser Profiles, 90
browsers, 87
    defining, 89-90
        multiple, 90
    names, modifying, 90
    previewing pages in, 33
    primary, 88-89
    removing, 90
    rendering colors, 40
    secondary, 89
    testing, 90-92
    triggering actions with, 96
buttons
    Get, 117
    Help (Property inspector), 9
    Put, 115, 119
    Replay, 123
    Report Settings, 111
    Right Alignment (Property inspector), 122
    Save As Command, 124
    Save Report, 112
    Site Map, 26
    View Options, 107

C

Cascading Style Sheets. *See* CSS
cells
    fixed, 84
    inserting, 83
    Property inspector, 83-84
Change Link Sitewide command, 118
Characters panel, 10-11
Check links action, 141
Check spelling shortcut, 143
Check Target Browsers, 90, 92
checking, links, shortcut, 144
Choose Spacer Image dialog box, 85
Circle tool, 66
Clean Up FrontPage HTML Code Sitewide extension, 26
Clean Up FrontPage HTML Sitewide extension, 19
CleanupFPHtml.mxp, 26
Clear action, 142

clip art, editable, 111
Close, Property inspector, shortcut, 143
Close action, 141
Code view, 34
    Roundtrip HTML, 4-5
codes
    deleting, 19, 26-29
    formatting, 28
    Roundtrip HTML, 4
    testing, 90
        errors, 92
        errors reports, 92
Color dialog box, 41
color picker, 40
color swatch (Property inspector), 8
color swatch control, 39
colors
    common, 40
    fonts, 39
    pages, background, 28
    rendered in browsers, 40
columns
    creating, using background images, 64
    fixed, 84
    width, modifying, 85
commands
    Change Link Sitewide, 118
    creating, 125
    Manage Extensions, 20
Copy, 142
Copy File As dialog box (Dreamweaver), 54
Copy HTML command, 42
copying, text, 42
    shortcut, 143
creating
    custom commands, 124-125
    editable regions, 106-108
    image maps, 65-66
    Library items (Dreamweaver), 99-100
    named anchors, 76-78
    pages, using templates, 108-110
    pages (Dreamweaver), 29
    paragraphs, shortcut, 143
    rollovers, 61-62
    tables, 79
        nested, 82-83
        using Layout view, 82-83
    templates, 105-106
        from existing pages, 105-106
CSS (Cascading Style Sheets), 47
    external style sheets, 48-50
    file naming, 49
    internal style sheets, 48
    modifying text, 47
    options, 28
custom commands
    creating, 124-125
    deleting, 125
    renaming, 125
customizing, Launcher, 13-14
Cut action, 142
cutting, text, 42

D

Define Sites dialog box, 25
defining
    browsers, 89-90
    Library items (Dreamweaver), 99-101
deleting
    behaviors (Dreamweaver), 96-97
    code, 19, 26-29
    custom commands, 125
design, Roundtrip HTML, 4
Design view, 34
    Roundtrip HTML, 4-5
    shortcut, 143
dialog boxes
    Add Browser, 89
    Choose Spacer Image, 85
    Copy File As, 54
    Include Dependent Files, 117
    Insert Email Link, 76
    Named Anchor, 77
    Page Properties, 79
    Popup Message, 94
    Reports, 111
    Rollover Image, 61
    Save As Command, 124
    Save As Template, 106
    Select Browser, 89
    Select File, 54
    Select Image Source, 109
    Update Library Items, 102
    Update Pages, 102-103
    Update Templates, 110
displaying, attributes, 57
Download Stats, (Status bar), 6
downloading, files, 117
Dreamweaver
    installing extensions, 20-21
    migrating from FrontPage, 19
Dreamweaver Exchange
    accessing, 20
    available extensions, 125

E

e-mail, sending with e-mail links, 75
e-mail links, 73-75. *See also* links
    previewing, 76
Edit Style Sheet dialog box, 49
editable regions, creating, 106-108
editing
    links, 144
    shortcuts, 142
    style sheets, shortcut, 144
    text, 142
elements
    inserting, 101-102
    updating, 99
error reports, 92
events, 93
    modifying, 95-96
Exit/Quit action, 141
exporting, Word files in HTML format, 43
Extension Manager, 20
extensions, 125

INDEX

Clean Up FrontPage HTML Code Sitewide, 26
Clean Up FrontPage HTML Sitewide, 19
CleanUpFPHtml.mxp, 21, 26
downloading from Dreamweaver Exchange, 20
filenames, 20
FPSiteImport.mxp, 20
FrontPage Site Import, 22
Import FrontPAge Site Wizard, 19
installing, 20-21
Publish Web Command, 19
Site Summary Reports, 19
SiteSummaryReports, 111
SiteSummaryReports.mxp, 21
Extensions Disclaimer dialog box, 21

F

file formats
    GIF, 53, 85
    JPEG, 53
    PNG, 53
filenames, extensions, 20
files
    downloading, 117
    getting, 115-117
    importing, 43-45
    putting, 115-116
    saving, 54
    transferring, 23, 115-117
    updated, uploading, 119
    uploading, 115-116
        to sites, 115
Find and Replace, 142
Find Next, 142
Fireworks, using editable clip art, 111
fixed cells, 84
fixed columns, 84
Flash buttons, inserting, 68-69
Flash content, on the Web, 68-69
Flash movies, inserting, 141
folders
    local site root, 21
    remote site root, 21
Font Size list, 38
fonts
    colors, 39
        choosing, 39
        modifying, 40-41
    families, changing, 37
    modifying, 37
    sizes
        absolute, 37-38
        choosing, 39
        choosing absolutes, 37
        decreasing, 39
        identifying, 39
        increasing, 39
        relative, 37
    sizing, (basefont) tag, 38

foreground graphics, 53-55, 63
formatting
    code, 28
    images, 53
    shortcut, 144
    text, 31, 36, 143
        Property inspector, 36
Forms panel, 10
    Characters panel, 10
FPSiteImport.mxp, 20
Frames panel, 10
    Characters panel, 10
FrontPage Migration Kit, 111-113
FrontPage Site Import extension, 22

G-H

Get button, 117
GIFs, 85
graphics
    background, 53, 63-65
    foreground, 53-55, 63
    inline, 53
    inserting, 53-56
    sorting, 56

Head panel, 11
    Characters panel, 11
headings (HTML)
    sizes, 31-33
    styles, 31
help, 144
Help button (Property inspector), 9
Help menu, 15-16
History panel, 121
    automating tasks, 121-124
        saving as commands, 124-125
        undo, 124
    commands, tracking, 122
    features
        limitations, 121
        replay, 121
    Save As Command button, 124
hotspots. *See* image maps
HTML
    converting from Word, 43
    exported from Word files, 43
    line spacing, 34
    Objects panel, 11-13
    Roundtrip. *See* Roundtrip HTML
    styles
        applying, 46-47
        clearing, 47
        paragraph, 45
        selection, 45
HTML Styles panel, 46

I

icons, Point-to-File, 9
image maps, 65
    creating, 65-66
    modifying, 66-67
    outlining, 67
    tools, 65-68
images. *See also* graphics
    aligning, 58
    formatting, 53
    inserting, 141
    naming, 57
        Javascript, 58
    optimizing for the Web, 62
    resizing, 58
Import FrontPage Site Wizard extension, 19
Import Word HTML dialog box, 44
importing
    files, 43-45
    Word files into Dreamweaver, 43
Include Dependent Files dialog box, 117
indenting text, shortcut, 144
inline graphics, 53
Insert Email Link dialog box, 76
Insert Image objects, 53-55
inserting
    background graphics, 63-64
    cells, 83
    e-mail links, 75-76
    elements, 101-102
    Flash buttons, 68-69
    Flash movies, 141
    graphics, 53-56
    images, 141
    Library items (Dreamweaver), 101
    line breaks, 143
    links
        e-mail, 75-76
        using Point-to-File, 78
    named anchors, 141
    nonbreaking space, 143
    objects, 141
    Shockwave Director movies, 141
    tables, 141
    tracing images, 79-80
Invisible Elements, setting, 36
italic text, shortcut, 144

J–L

JavaScript names, 58

Launcher (Status bar), 6-8
    customizing, 13-14
layout, previewing, 88
    Site window, 88
Layout view, 80
    tables, creating, 82-83
Library folders, 99
Library items (Dreamweaver)
    creating, 99-100
    defining, 99-101
    inserting, 101
    managing, 99
    modifying, 101-102. *See also* Library elements (Dreamweaver)
    storing, 100
    updating, 99, 103-104
line break (br) tags, 35
line breaks, inserting, 143
line spacing, 34
Link Field, 58
links
    absolute, 73
        updating, 118
    broken, 73
    checking, shortcut, 144
    creating, using Property inspector, 73-74
    e-mail, 73-75
        inserting, 75-76
    editing, 144
    mailto, 118
    modifying, on multiple pages, 118
    relative, 73
        Point-to-File feature, 74
        updating, 118
    removing, shortcut, 144. *See also* URLs (Uniform Resource Locators)
    to files, 74
    to named anchors, 76-78
    updating, 118
        on multiple pages, 118
local site root folder, 21
locked regions, 106

M

macros. *See* actions
mailto links, 76. *See also* e-mail links
    updating, 118
Manage Extensions command, 20
managing
    Library items (Dreamweaver), 99
    sites, 21
margin controls, 60
margins (tables), removing, 86
menus, Help, 15-16
meta tags, 99
Microsoft Word. *See* Word
migrating, to Dreamweaver, 19
modifying
    attributes, using Property inspector, 57
    behaviors (Dreamweaver), 96-97
    browsers
        names, 90
        Primary, 90
        Secondary, 90
    column width, 85
    events, 95-96
    fonts, 37
        colors, 40-41
    font families, 37
    image maps, 66-67
    Library items (Dreamweaver), 101-102
    links, 118
    tables, using Layout view, 80-82
    tag source, using Property inspector, 57
    text, 36

INDEX

moving
    objects, shortcut, 143
    text, 143

N

Named Anchor dialog box, 77
Named Anchor symbol, 77
named anchors, 76
    creating, 76-78
    HTML, 73
    inserting, 141
    linking to, 76-78
naming
    images, 57
    sites (Dreamweaver), 22
    templates, 106
nested tables, creating, 82-83
New document action, 141
New Editable Region option, 107
no access symbol, 109
nonbreaking spaces, 34
    inserting, 35
        shortcut, 143

O

objects
    inserting, 141
    moving, 143
    outlining, 67
Objects panel, 9, 100
    Characters panel, 10-11
    Common panel, 10
    HTML elements, 11-13
    Special panel, 11
Office HTML Filter 2.0, 44
Open action, Property inspector, 143
Open an HTML file action, 141
Open in frame action, 141
opening pages (Dreamweaver), 29
Optimize command
    cropping, images, 63
    modifying
        file types, 63
        number of colors, 63
optimizing images, for the Web, 62
organizing sites, 19
outdenting text, 144

P

Page Properties dialog box, 79
pages
    background colors, 28
    creating, using templates, 108-110
    previewing, 109
    previewing in your browser, 33
    updating, 101
pages (Dreamweaver)
    creating, 29-30
    new, opening, 29

panels
    Assets, 56, 99
    Behaviors, 93, 98
    History, 121
    Objects, 100
    viewing, 142
paragraph tags, 33
paragraphs
    creating, 143
    line space between, 34
    text, adding, 33-34
    word-wrap, 33
Paste, 142
Paste HTML command, 42
pasting text, 42
Point-to-File
    feature, 74
    icon, 9
    links, inserting, 78
Polygon tool, 67
Popup Message dialog box, 94
Preferences, 142
Preview in Browser feature, 87
    layout, previewing, 88
previewing
    e-mail links, 76
    layout, 88
        using Browser Profiles, 90
        using Preview Using Local
            Server option, 90
    pages, 109
primary browsers, 88-89
productivity, increasing with
    History panel, 121
    Library elements, 99
Professional QuickStart Collection, 111
Property inspector, 8, 31, 55
    attributes
        displaying, 57
        modifying, 57
    cells, 83-84
    choosing font sizes, 39
    color swatch, 8
    creating
        image maps, 65
        links, 73-74
    e-mail links, inserting, 76
    fonts, choosing absolutes, 38
    Help button, 9
    image parameters, 57-59
    Point-to-File icon, 9
    Quick Tag Editor, 9
    Right alignment button, 122
    tables, 83-84
    text, formatting, 36
Publish Web Command extension, 19
PublishWebCommand.mxp, 21
Put button, 115, 119
putting files, 115-116
    Put button, 115

Q–R

Quick Tag Editor, (Property inspector), 9

Rectangle tool, 66
Redo, 142
Reference panel, 16-17
relative font sizes, 37
relative links, 73
    Point-to-File feature, 74
remote site root folder, 21
removing
    browsers, 90
    links, 144
renaming, custom commands, 125
replay, using, 121
Replay button, 123
Report dialog box (Dreamweaver), 26
Report Settings button, 111
reports
    accessing problems, 105
    outputting, 19
    Results, 29
    Results window, 112
    running, 111-113
Reports dialog box, 111
resizing, images, 58
Results dialog box, 29
Results reports, 29
Right alignment button (Property inspector), 122
Rollover Image dialog box, 61
rollovers
    creating, 61-62
    definition, 61
Roundtrip HTML, 4
    Code view, 4-5
    Design view, 4-5

S

Save action, 141
Save as action, 141
Save As Command button (History panel), 124
Save As Command dialog box, 124
Save As Template dialog box, 106
Save Report button, 112
saving
    actions, 124-125
    automated tasks, as commands, 124-125
    files, 54
secondary browsers, 89
Select All, 142
Select Browser dialog box, 89
Select File dialog box (Dreamweaver), 54
Select Image Source dialog box, 109
Select Style File dialog box, 48
selecting
    text, Tag Selector, 37
    words, shortcut, 143
servers (FrontPage), connecting to, 19
Set Background Color option, 28
Shockwave Director movies, inserting, 141

shortcuts
    Check links, 141
    Close, 141
    creating, pages (Dreamweaver), 30
    editing, 142
    Exit/Quit, 141
    formatting, 144
    inserting objects, 141
    New document, 141
    Open an HTML file, 141
    Open in frame, 141
    opening a file dialog box, 20
    Save, 141
    Save As, 141
    text, aligning, 42
    undo, 35
Show Log on Completion option, 45
Site Map button, 26
Site Summary Reports extension, 19
Site window (Dreamweaver), previewing layout, 88
sites
    getting files, 115
    links
        modifying, 118
        updating, 118
    Macromedia support, 126
    managing, 21
    obtaining information, 25
    organizing, 19
    original files, getting, 117
    putting files, 115
    updating, 103-104
    uploading files to, 115
sites (Dreamweaver)
    creating, 22-24
    definition, 21
    naming, 22. *See also* Webs (FrontPage)
    viewing, 24
SiteSummaryReports extension, 111
SiteSummaryReports.mxp, 21
sizes, absolute fonts, 38
sorting
    graphics, 56
    images, 56
source field. *See* Src field
spacers, 85-86
spaces, nonbreaking, 34
spacing, adjusting, 35
Split code view button, 34
Src (source) field, 58
Status bar, 5
    Download Stats, 6
    Launcher, 6-8
    Tag Selector, 6-7
    Window Sizer, 6
storing, Library items (Dreamweaver), 100
Style Sheet dialog box, 49
style sheets, editing, 144
summary reports, 19
symbols
    Named Anchor, 77
    no access, 109

INDEX

T

tables
    creating, 79
    inserting, 141
    margins, removing, 86
    modifying, using Layout view, 80-82
    nested, creating, 82-83
    Property inspector, 83-84
    spacers, 85
Tag Selector, 6-7, 37
tags
      , 34
    deleting, Import Word HTML command, 44
    line break (br), 35
    paragraphs, 33
    selecting, using Tag Selector, 37
    shortcuts, 33
tasks
    automating, 121-125
    repeating, 123
templates, 106
    creating, 105-106
        from existing pages, 105-106
    creating pages, 108-110
    distinguishing, 106
    editable regions, 106
        creating, 106-108
    FrontPage versus Dreamweaver, 105
    locked regions, 106
    Macromedia, 111
    managing, using Assets panel, 108
    naming, 106
    Professional QuickStart Collection, 111
    third-party, 111
    updating, 110
Templates folders, 105
testing
    behaviors (Dreamweaver), 95
    browsers, 90-92
    codes, 90
text
    aligning, 41
        keyboard shortcuts, 42
        shortcut, 144
        using keyboard shortcuts, 41
        using menu commands, 41
        using Property inspector, 41
    bold, shortcut 144
    copying, 42, 143
    creating, 70
    cutting, 42
    editing, 142
    font families, 37
    formatting, 31, 36, 143
    headings (HTML), sizes, 31-33
    indenting, shortcut, 144
    italic, shortcut, 144
    modifying, 36
    moving, shortcut, 143
    outdenting, shortcut, 144
    pasting, 42
    underlining, 42

Text Property inspector, 8
toolbars, 3
tracing images
    definition, 79
    inserting, 79-80
tracking commands, using History panel, 122
transferring files, 23, 115-117. *See also* putting files

U

underlined text, 42
Undo, 142
undo shortcut, 35
unlocked regions. *See* editable regions
Update Library Items dialog box, 102
Update Pages dialog box, 102-103
Update Templates dialog box, 110
updating
    elements, on Web pages, 99
    Library items (Dreamweaver), 103-104
    links, 118
    pages, 101
    results of, 104
    sites, 103-104
    templates, 110
uploading files, 115-116
    Put button, 119
    updated, 119
URLs (Uniform Resource Locators), 73

V–Z

View Options button, 107
viewing
    assets, 56
    panels, 142
    sites (Dreamweaver), 24
views
    Code, 34
    Design, 34, 143

Webs (FrontPage), 21
Welcome panel, 14
Welcome screen, 14
Window Sizer (Status bar), 6
Word, converting files to HTML, 43
Word files, importing into Dreamweaver, 43
words, selecting, 143

Read This Before Opening the Software

By opening this package, you are agreeing to be bound by the following agreement:

Some of the software included with this product may be copyrighted, in which case all rights are reserved by the respective copyright holder. You are licensed to use software copyrighted by the publisher and its licensors on a single computer. You may copy and/or modify the software as needed to facilitate your use of it on a single computer. Making copies of the software for any other purpose is a violation of the United States copyright laws.

This software is sold as is without warranty of any kind, either expressed or implied, including but not limited to the implied warranties of merchantability and fitness for a particular purpose. Neither the publisher nor its dealers or distributors assumes any liability for any alleged or actual damages arising from the use of this program. (Some states do not allow for the exclusion of implied warranties, so the exclusion might not apply to you.)